Cross-Cultural Theology

Western Reflections in Asia

Daniel J. Adams

John Knox Press
ATLANTA

Acknowledgment is made for permission to edit and reprint articles by the author from the following publications:

To *Ching Feng* for "Matteo Ricci and the New China," *Ching Feng* 23, no. 2 (1980), used by permission. (chapter 2)

To *The East Asia Journal of Theology* for "Methodology and the Search for a New Spirituality," *The South East Asia Journal of Theology* 18, no. 2 (1977), used by permission. (chapter 3)

To *Shepherd's Staff* for "The Importance of Christian Myth," no. 42 (June 1975); for "Theology as Grammar: Reflections on the Thought of Ludwig Wittgenstein," no. 43 (June 1976); and for "The Theologian as a Caring Person," no. 45 (June 1978). Used by permission. (chapters 8, 4, and 1 respectively)

To the *Taiwan Journal of Theology* for "The Ethics of Church Unity: A Philosophical Perspective," no. 2 (March 1980); for "Theological Method: Four Contemporary Models," no. 3 (March 1981); and for "The Rational and the Mystical in Theological Construction," no. 4 (March 1982). Used by permission. (chapters 6, 7, and 9 respectively)

To the Taiwan Theological College for "Toward an Asian Hermeneutic" in Daniel J. Adams, *Biblical Hermeneutics: An Introduction*, Taiwan Theological College/March Publications, 1976. (chapter 5)

Acknowledgment is made for permission to quote from the following sources:

To Baker Book House for excerpt from Norman L. Geisler, "Some Philosophical Perspectives on Missionary Dialogue" in *Theology and Mission*, copyright 1978 by Baker Book House.

Library of Congress Cataloging-in-Publication Data
    Adams, Daniel J.
      Cross-cultural theology.

      1. Theology—Methodology.   2. Theology, Doctrinal—
Asia. I. Title.
BR118.A23   1987   230'.01   87-17140
ISBN 0-8042-0685-6

Preface

The essays in this volume were written between 1974 and 1984. During this decade the author served on the faculties of Taiwan Theological College in Taipei, Taiwan, and of Hanil Theological Seminary in Chonju, Korea. While in Taiwan he was also a member of the faculty of the South East Asia Graduate School of Theology. Most of these essays have been previously published in journals of limited circulation; they are being presented in book format to make them more widely available.

Although written in Asia, these essays do not pretend to be Asian theology, for the writer is western by birth and education. The task of writing Asian theology quite properly belongs to Asians, not to expatriate Americans and Europeans. At the same time, the ideas contained herein were developed within the Asian context and this makes them somewhat unique, for it is inevitable that eastern and western thought have come together into one stream. The result is a blending of east and west into a cross-cultural theology.

At first glance the subject matter of these essays appears to be quite diverse, especially if each is taken separately. Taken together, however, a common theme of theological method emerges. As such, this collection of essays contributes to the ongoing task of clarifying and refining theological methodology. It is presented to you the reader with the hope that you will be stimulated to reexamine your theological presuppositions. This in turn will deepen your understanding of the Word and sharpen your proclamation of that same Word.

The reader will notice that these essays deal with Asia in general and with Chinese culture in particular, while Korea is mentioned only in passing. The reason for this is not to slight Korea; rather, a collection of essays dealing only with Korea is planned for a later volume.

Special thanks is due to Dr. Ching-fen Hsiao, past President of Tainan Theological College in Tainan, Taiwan, for making available to the author his personal typewriter as well as providing a room in Alumni Hall in which to live and work during the author's stay in Tainan in January of 1985. The kind hospitality of the faculty and students at Tainan Theological College will long be remembered by the author and his wife; they helped to make our period of study and research most enjoyable.

This work could not have been published without the encouragement of Clifton Kirkpatrick, Insik Kim, and Harry Phillips of the Division of International Mission of the Presbyterian Church (U.S.A.). Walter Sutton, Joan Crawford, and Patricia H. Sprinkle of John Knox Press were most helpful in the process of transforming a typewritten manuscript into a published book. Herbert Schaefer of the Lutheran Theological Seminary in Hong Kong arranged for the use of a computer which greatly simplified the process of revision and rewriting. To all of these persons I am most grateful.

The suggestion that these essays be collected together and published in this volume came from my wife and colleague in ministry, the Rev. Carol Fang-lan Chou, and to her I owe my deepest gratitude.

Daniel J. Adams
Hanil Theological Seminary
Chonju, North Cholla
Korea

Contents

To my theological teachers
at the
University of Dubuque Theological Seminary

Donald G. Bloesch

Carnegie Samuel Calian

Arthur C. Cochrane

Introduction

The task of thinking and doing theology has occupied humankind since the dawn of human consciousness. Early efforts at theological construction were localized, largely concerned with finding an explanation for the trials and tribulations of life. Gradually attempts were made to structure reality into an overall religious framework. With the rise of the great world religions, theological work became even more structured and comprehensive, and theological systems began to appear. As western civilization, and Christianity, began to expand and develop, Christian theology in its western systematized form began to be accepted as universal. This theology was extended throughout the world as *the* theology. Christians in every culture of the world studied this theology and used it as a model for their own theological work.

In recent years, however, a great change has taken place. Christians throughout the world are rediscovering—or, in some cases, discovering for the first time—their own religious and cultural roots. They are realizing that here, in their own cultures and their own languages, are the building blocks out of which theology can be constructed. As a result, many are questioning the universality of western theological systems. Furthermore, with issues of social, economic, and political justice increasingly coming to the fore as matters of theological concern, ever-increasing numbers of Christians are becoming dissatisfied with western tendencies toward abstract conceptualization. The result of all this ferment is that numerous issue-oriented theologies and local theologies are springing up, theologies which speak to the needs of unique cultural and historical contexts.

Asia today provides a dramatic, exciting example. Here two of the world's great religions—Hinduism and Buddhism—coexist with national religions such as Shinto and cultural religions such as the Folk Religion of Taiwan. New religious movements like the Unification Church and Won Buddhism and secular, quasi-religious movements—Marxism, materialism, and the ideology of anti-communism—confront two missionary religions with origins in the Middle East: Christianity and Islam. Islam moved eastward across the mountain ranges of central Asia while Christianity was moving westward through Europe, across North America, and across the Pacific to Asia. Within this matrix of almost unbelievable pluralism, contemporary Christian theology is being thought out, written down, and put into practice.

This matrix involves much, much more than religious factors, however, for Asia is struggling for cultural identity in the midst of a legacy of colonialism and proxy wars fought by superpowers on Asian soil. Asia is an area of enormous poverty and economic exploitation coupled with vast reserves of natural resources and literally billions of people striving for that elusive goal of development. Asia claims the world's oldest civilizations with the most stable social systems known to humankind, yet Asia has also undergone countless wars and rebellions, and its social systems perpetuate such injustices as the caste system and discrimination against women. Asia has evolved political systems that have existed for centuries, yet an increasing number of countries view a military dictatorship as the most expedient solution to political upheaval. In the midst of these problems, all of which are crying out for solution, creative and solid theological work is being done.

The essays in this book were all written within the Asian context and with that context in mind. They are, of course, not Asian theology but neither are they, strictly speaking, western theology either. They are, quite simply, a few observations about theological method written by an expatriate living and working in Asia.

I begin with a brief consideration of the theologian as a person. What kind of person should the theologian be? What should be his or her concerns in carrying out theological work? Although this list is by no means exhaustive, I conclude that the theologian should care about humanity as the concern of theology, the knowledge of God as the definition of theology, the church as the context of theology, and the search for truth as the task of theology.

The theologian should, therefore, be able to do theology in the concrete—that is, within a real-life situation. To suggest how this should be done I consider the life and work of that remarkable sixteenth-century Jesuit missionary to China, Matteo Ricci. His theological style models some ways theology might best be done in the context of modern China.

Spirituality is an element that is often neglected when considering theological method. Sadly, it is also an aspect of the theologian's life that is, in all too many instances, missing. How can one develop a form of spirituality that is both Christian and at the same time deeply rooted in one's own culture and tradition? The experiential approach toward spirituality evidenced by the life and work of Thomas Merton provide one approach to spirituality that could apply within Asia's religious pluralism.

The question of language and its use or misuse in theology has long been a topic of interest to philosophers. One of the most creative philosophers in this field was Ludwig Wittgenstein. Although he wrote very little pertaining directly to theology, what he did write was highly significant. Nowhere is theological language more important than in a linguistic Babel such as Asia, and Wittgenstein provides several helpful insights for the theologian interested in communicating the Christian faith in this kind of situation. Language can also serve as a useful model in attempting to understand other religions, since religion, like language, is based upon common human behavior patterns.

One cannot speak of language without becoming concerned with questions relating to the interpretation of Scripture. Hermeneutics, or the principles of textual interpretation, is often thought of as being western in origin, but nothing could be further from the truth; indeed, hermeneutics has a long and venerable history in Asia, and modern Asian theologians have made significant contributions to hermeneutics. I consider three of them; Kazoh Kitamori and the theology of the pain of God, Kosuke Koyama and water buffalo theology, and Emerito Nacpil and the Critical Asian Principle. All three were innovators in developing uniquely Asian principles of biblical interpretation.

Presbyterian-Reformed churches are notorious for their differences when it comes to biblical interpretation, differences that often result in denominational schism. It is worth asking, therefore, why the Presbyterian Church in Taiwan, which is ethnically, linguistically, and politically divided, is not also ecclesiastically divided. In the face of seemingly insurmountable odds this church has maintained its unity through the years. Among the factors that play a significant role are cultural and philosophical beliefs common to the Chinese. I suggest how western churches in their elusive quest for unity can learn from the example of the Presbyterian Church in Taiwan.

Moving from the practical arena of church unity to that of theological methodology, I consider four ways of doing theology: systematic theology, philosophical theology, political theology, and contextual theology. For each method covered I present one model as a working example: G. C. Berkouwer as a model for doing systematic theology, John B. Cobb, Jr. and process theology as a model for doing philosophical theology, Robert McAfee Brown and liberation theology as a model for doing political theology, and C. S. Song as a model for doing contextual theology. Taken together, these four methodologies and models summarize the major theological options currently available on the Asian scene.

Theology is usually considered to be a rational enterprise, but within the Asian context one cannot avoid confrontation with the mythical worldview. Although there are numerous attempts to excise myth from the realm of Christian discourse, the fact remains that for many people, including Christians, myth is very much a part of reality. The Bible, too, contains numerous examples of the mythical. I contend that myth is important, that without it the very soul of the Christian gospel is lost. Theological work, therefore, must provide for the inclusion of Christian myth. The work of C. S. Lewis provides helpful insights for theologians working in this area.

Asia characteristically views relationships between opposites as dipolar, summed up in the words "both/and," while the West tends to view reality in dualistic terms, summed up in the words "either/or." Unfortunately, western dualism has been introduced to Asia where it exercises considerable influence in the Asian church. Two significant breakthroughs in scientific discovery, however, offer hope of restoring the dipolar view: research into the nature and function of the two hemispheres of the human brain, and high energy particle physics. Findings in both fields tend to support the dipolar view over against the dualistic view. Theologically it is inappropriate to speak of the sacred and the secular, contemplation and action, or evangelism and social action as if they were mutually exclusive categories of reality. Rather, they are dipolar aspects of the same reality, somewhat like the positive and negative poles of a magnet. Theologically, the rational and the mystical, which are often seen in terms of "either/or" categories, are held together in creative relationship in the doctrine of Word and Sacrament, a doctrine which needs to be reemphasized in the theological life and work of the church.

I conclude this collection of essays with some suggestions for thinking and doing theology in the future, within a global and pluralistic context which will necessitate a bringing together of the universal and the particular. I believe that contextual theologies, including those of the West, must come together so that common elements may be discerned and a global theology constructed. This will not be a universal theology in the sense of imperialistic western theologies of the past. Rather, it will develop out of particular contextual theologies so that the universal and the particular may engage in creative interaction. Perhaps most important, this theology will be a theology in process—as the Reformers would say, constantly being reformed. This kind of theology will be able to speak to the people of Asia with their many cultures, languages, and social systems. And this kind of theology can speak to the people of the West as well. These essays are presented to the reader in the hope that they might contribute in some small way to the thinking and doing of theology in today's world.

1

The Theologian as
a Caring Person

The theological task of thinking and doing quite properly begins with the theologian. What kind of a person is the theologian? During the Middle Ages theologians were the scholars of their age who wrote books, founded universities, engaged in lengthy disputations on seemingly abstract subjects, and conversed together in that universal language of the church, Latin. The theologians of the Reformation, on the other hand, were often outstanding preachers who presented eloquent sermons in the vernacular. Some were even radical revolutionaries who challenged not only ecclesiastical tradition but social convention as well. Today, theologians are apt to be denominational executives or members of international ecumenical bodies such as the Lutheran World Federation, the World Alliance of Reformed Churches, or the World Council of Churches.

In the past, theologians were almost always male and were certain to be members of the ordained clergy. Present-day theologians, however, include both men and women among their ranks. Furthermore, a growing number of astute laypersons are making significant contributions to the theological task. Indeed, in the Eastern Orthodox Church many theologians have been lay members of theological faculties in the universities. Theologians, then, represent a great variety of people, but the question still remains:.what kind of person is the theologian?

The Place of the Theologian

The theologian occupies a rather unique position in the community of faith. On the one hand, the theologian is considered necessary for the life and work of the church, to teach in the church's theological colleges and seminaries and to write books which pastors use in the preparation of sermons. The importance of the theologian is demonstrated by the fact that literally thousands of pastors are returning to theological colleges and seminaries each year for various kinds of continuing education programs. This clearly demonstrates that the theologian has something of significance to offer the church.

At the same time, however, the theologian is often misunderstood. We sometimes hear statements like "At the theological college they are teaching new theology," or "I hear that those theologians are very liberal," and "Those theologians are dangerous—they raise doubts and questions which cause people to lose their faith." The implication behind these statements seems to be that theology, or at least the theologian, is not good for the church and that theologians are trying to destroy the very faith which pastors are seeking to build up. One also hears statements to the effect that theologians are "ivory tower thinkers who care little for the day-to-day activities of the church." Theologians are accused of using language which ordinary church people cannot understand, and when asked to preach in a local church or speak at a conference or retreat, their presentation is sometimes perceived as being virtually incomprehensible to an audience of lay persons.

These misunderstandings are quite serious, for they drive a wedge between the theological college and the church, a wedge which causes distrust among members of the community of faith and severely hinders the proclamation of the gospel. Such a situation takes on critical significance in most Asian societies, where the Christian population is so small that it cannot afford to be divided. Hence, it is vitally important that the church be quite clear concerning the theologian's life and work:

what a theologian does and what a theologian is concerned about.

I shall consider four areas of caring and concern which arise out of four different communities in which the theologian finds himself or herself. This is by no means an exhaustive list, but it does provide a foundation upon which to build. These areas of caring and concern are as follows: (1) humanity as the *concern* of theology, arising out of the fact that the theologian is a member of the human community; (2) the knowledge of God as the *definition* of theology, arising out of the fact that the theologian is a member of the believing community; (3) the church as the *context* of theology, arising out of the fact that the theologian is a member of the Christian community; and (4) the search for truth as the *task* of theology, arising out of the fact that the theologian is a member of the learning community. The theologian's concerns and task, therefore, are a direct response to the needs that arise out of the various communities in which theologians live and work.

Humanity as the Concern of Theology

The theologian is first and foremost a member of the human community. This is, of course, an obvious statement, but when carefully considered it can have disturbing implications for some Christians. The theologian is a human being before he or she is a Christian, a Korean, a Presbyterian, a man or woman, a conservative or liberal, a layperson or pastor. The first community in which we all hold membership is the human community, and this human community transcends all cultural, religious, racial, political, and social boundaries. Unfortunately, this is all too easy to forget, especially when involved in defending various doctrinal interpretations of the Christian faith. "Christians frequently launch into 'the defence of the right doctrines' so passionately and energetically that they become Christ*ianity* and cease to be Christ*ians*."[1] We need to be reminded that only Christ*ians* are people; Christ*ianity* is a collection of ideas which have no meaning whatsoever once they are divorced from the realm of human discourse. We are first of all human persons; only then are we Christians. The theologian is one with all humanity and shares humanity's hopes, desires, fears, frustrations, and aspirations. This fact has several important ramifications for the theologian.

First, theology as a discipline is human work. "Theology is done by humans for human purposes; theological work must be assessed by human standards, and its judges are themselves always ordinary human beings."[2] The concern of the theologian is humanity and the work of the theologian is carried out by human beings for distinctly human purposes. This point cannot be overemphasized, for it means that theology is conditioned by human culture and history. It means that theology is always in process and is pluralistic in nature; there is no one theology, but rather many theologies, each reflecting its unique culture and history. It also means that theology, like all other human enterprises, is both fallible and tainted by sin. Perhaps most significant of all, it means that the task of the theologian is never completed, for human cultural and historical development is a continuing process.

Second, theology is an attempt to reflect upon and to understand human religious experience, especially as this experience touches upon the transcendent. Even in the case of divine revelation, theology is still a human attempt to understand that revelation. "Every human society is an enterprise of world-building. Religion occupies a distinctive place in this enterprise."[3] Religion is a part of what it means to be human, so theology, therefore, forms a vital part of our social construction of reality. It is for this reason that we humans make statements of faith, compose creeds and confessions, and write endless religious books and pamphlets. This is our way of classifying and organizing our thinking about God and religious experience, which we do both for our own personal benefit and for the benefit of others. God does not benefit from Karl Barth's thirteen volume *Church Dogmatics,* nor is God going to read C. S. Song's *Third-Eye Theology.* These books were written for humans to read, discuss, and understand. "Theology is a very human business, a craft, and sometimes an art."[4] Theology is by and for humans, even when we include the words "to the glory of God."

Finally, theology deals with the human situation in all of its fullness.

> The "situation" theology must consider is the creative interpretation of existence, an interpretation which is carried on in every period of history under all kinds of psychological and sociological conditions. . . . The "situation" to which theology must respond is the totality of man's creative self-interpretation in a special period.[5]

Tillich is speaking here of the human situation, of human existence, of human interpretation, of human history, and of human psychological and sociological conditions. Theology is not concerned with the social structure of heaven, the psychology of angels, the historical development of demons, and the nature of the pre-existent Christ one million years before the birth of Jesus. However, theology is concerned with death and human destiny (and therefore about heaven); theology is concerned about evil and human nature (and thus about demons and the demonic); and theology is concerned about the reality and nature of being (and hence with angels and the pre-existence of Christ). The real concern of theology is humanity. The life and work of the theologian is focused first of all around that concern.

The Knowledge of God
as the Definition of Theology

The theologian is a member of the believing community, and as such he or she begins with an affirmation of belief. This belief asserts, first of all, that the universe is a cosmos and not chaos.

> Religion implies the farthest reach of man's self-externalization, of his infusion of reality with his own meanings. Religion implies that human order is projected into the totality of being. Put differently, religion is the audacious attempt to conceive of the entire universe as being humanly significant.[6]

In addition, this belief which the theologian affirms includes the idea of a being whom we call God who is somehow responsible for the order which we find in the universe. The precise definitions of God are many, but no matter how God is defined, all theologians by virtue of the definition of theology—knowledge of God or discourse about God—affirm a belief in such a being. Kaufman: "The proper business of theology (theos-logos) is the analysis, criticism and reconstruction of the concept of God."[7] Barth: "The Church confesses God, by the fact that she speaks of God. . . . As a theological discipline, dogmatics is the scientific test to which the Christian Church puts herself regarding the language about God which is peculiar to her."[8] Thielicke: "A theological thought can breathe only in the atmosphere of dialogue with God."[9] The theologian, therefore, begins with a belief in God and in an orderly universe which has meaning.

It is important to point out that thus far I have said nothing concerning Jesus Christ; I have spoken only about God. The Christian theologian shares a universe of discourse with the non-Christian theologian which is of vital importance in Asia. Not only is the theologian a member of the human community, but he or she is also a member of the believing community, a community which includes Buddhists, Hindus, Jews, Muslims, Taoists, followers of folk and tribal religions, and members of various religious groups too numerous to be named. All believe in a God or gods, and all believe in an orderly and meaningful universe. The theologian, therefore, cares about those members of the believing community who are outside the Christian faith.

Because theology as I have defined it implies belief, the theologian is not merely a historian of religion who attempts to examine human religious behavior objectively. His or her belief in God has already given a subjective perspective to the study of religion. Nor is the theologian merely a philosopher of religion who attempts to describe God rationally, for belief implies that there are limits to human reason. The theologian may also be a historian of religion or a philosopher of religion, but first of all the theologian will be one who can affirm: "I believe in God."

As we think about some of the misconceptions which are commonly held concerning theologians, we would do well to remember that the theologian is also a believer who cares about God. It may very well be that the "new theology" which is so shocking when first heard is really a deep expression of the theologian's concern both for humanity as a whole and for the God whom we say loves that humanity. The theologian as a member of both the human community and the believing community feels a sense of concern toward these communities, a concern which must, by necessity, reach far beyond the confines of the Christian church. The so-called "new theology" may not speak directly to the community of Christians which we call the church, but it may speak to the community at large, the human and believing community, in ways that a more traditional theology could never do. It is imperative that we understand that the theologian has membership in communities other than the Christian church, and that he or she must speak to the needs which arise out of those other communities.

Theology is likewise a form of witness. The theologian not only believes, but also bears witness to that belief.

> To express this in another way, theology can never "prove" preaching, but
> it has the same outlook as preaching; it is also a witness, only with other
> methods and means. So its scientific character, its correct relation to its
> subject matter, its objectivity in the full sense of the word, is expressed
> only if it regards itself as a witness functioning through reflection.[10]

The theologian bears witness about faith in God to the world and is
therefore involved in the total mission of the believer. This aspect of
the theologian's work takes on added significance in the contemporary
world, for we live in an age of agnosticism, atheism, and secularism
where belief in God is either denied or ignored. It is the theologian's
unique task to speak to the world about God. The theologian is more
than a social worker, political revolutionary, or ethical humanist. The
theologian is a believer who must bear witness to the God "in whom
we live and move and have our being" (Acts 28:17).

The Church as the Context of Theology

The Christian theologian is a member of the Christian church. This
means that the Christian theologian believes within the context of those
who understand God to have been active in the life and ministry of
Jesus. This theologian is thus placed in a kind of paradoxical situation:
he or she is first of all a member of the human community and of the
believing community, yet he or she was probably nurtured and educated
within the Christian community and thus understands larger communities from the perspective of the Christian community. In a very real
sense then, the church becomes the most important community for the
Christian theologian in that it provides a worldview, a perspective, and
a conceptual framework with which to view reality. Therefore, the
church is the context of Christian theology. Henceforth, in speaking of
theologians, we shall be referring specifically to Christian theologians.

Theologians are agreed that "theology, as a function of the church,
must serve the needs of the church."[11] "Dogmatics is a theological discipline. But theology is a function of the church."[12] Although Tillich
and Barth are far apart in terms of theological systems and basic presuppositions, both affirm that the Church is the context of theology.
This means that theologians and pastors are directly related to each
other in terms of their Christian vocations. In the Christian community

the theologian confronts the pastor; the pastor confronts the theologian; together they confront the laity with the message of the gospel as they understand it. And, I should add, the entire church confronts, and is confronted by, the Word of God.

The church provides the historical context not only for theology, but also for the Bible, because the Bible is the written record of the community of faith as it has understood the gospel down through the ages. Indeed, the Bible was written, canonized, and interpreted by this community of faith. The Old Testament, of course, concerns itself with the Hebrew community of believers and not the Christian community, although the Hebrew community of faith can be seen as the predecessor of the Christian community found in the New Testament. This is a point which we Christians should never forget, especially as we seek to bear witness in a non-Christian environment. "The Bible, however, is the basic source of systematic theology because it is the original document about the events on which the Christian church is founded."[13] The life and work of the church is inseparably bound up with the biblical record and the two cannot be set apart from each other. Thus the theologian cares about the Bible, both as a historical record of the early church and as a source of data for theology.

For the theologian, the Christian church is much like a family. It is within the church that he or she finds an identity, for "the history of theology is the history of Christians and their decisions made in faith presented in the form of reflections which are the consequences of those decisions."[14] The church provides the theologian with a sense of history, with direction and hope for the future, and with meaning and mission for the present. It is part of the theologian's task to help the church articulate its message within given cultural and historical situations, and it is for this reason that the church, usually through its theologians, makes declarations, statements, and doctrinal formulas such as creeds and confessions. These statements and creeds then take their place among other historical records and so provide a sense of history and identity to present and future generations of Christians.

The theologian cares deeply about the church and its work, for he or she has been given the great responsibility for articulating the faith for this and coming generations. This is not an easy task. The theologian is not only the church's greatest supporter, but also its severest critic when the church has become slothful in its task. The theologian not only follows church doctrine and teaching, but is also responsible for providing leadership when old forms no longer properly convey the Christian message. The theologian not only brings healing to situations of division and strife but also wounds with judgment in cases where the church has become guilty of heresy, injustice, corruption, or oppression. In all these capacities, whether pleasant or unpleasant, the theologian acts as a caring member of the Christian community, the church.

In the words attributed to Martin Luther during those turbulent years of the Protestant Reformation: "The church may be a whore, but she is still our mother." Only one who cared deeply about the church could utter those words. Only one who had been nurtured by the church could speak with such judgment and tenderness. The theologian who is true to his or her calling is a loyal son or daughter of the church.

The Search for Truth as the Task of Theology

We have spoken of the concern of theology, the definition of theology, and the context of theology. We now turn to the task of theology which arises out of the fact that the theologian is a member of the learning community. One might be tempted to say that the theologian is part of the community of scholars, but not all theologians are members of theological faculties and not all theologians are scholars in the sense that they write numerous journal articles and books. All theologians are, however, members of the learning community in that they are searching for truth. Like all who search for truth, the theologian is concerned with the expansion of knowledge and understanding. With his or her colleagues in other disciplines, the theologian seeks to push the human mind to its limits, seeks to develop new concepts and ideas, and hopes to influence the direction of human thought and self-understanding. Thus it is crucial that the theologian be given the freedom which allows honesty and openness in this task. The theologian cannot function adequately in a church environment closed to that which is new and fearful of truth. The theologian must insist that all truth is God's truth, so there is no need to fear truth. The task given to the theologian is thus both exhilarating and filled with the anticipation of creative discovery.

The theologian seeks truth, not merely a restatement of old doctrines and teaching. The theologian understands theology to be dynamic and open-ended, not static and closed. There is an element of danger here, however, for this implies doubt and the unknown. "Every theological idea which makes an impression upon you must be regarded as a challenge to your faith."[15] It is obvious that many church members would have great difficulty living with this kind of uncertainty in their faith, and it is for this reason that theologians spend so many years in theological study. It is through years of advanced study that they are given the resources and tools which enable them to face doubt without losing their faith. And it is at this point that the theologian's membership in the Christian community and in the learning community are most likely to conflict. Indeed, he or she has been given this task by the church. As a Christian, however, the theologian must seek to build up the faith of the Christian community and must be careful not to sow doubt among those who have neither the educational nor intellectual resources to deal positively with doubt. It is here that the theologian is most often irresponsible and misunderstood. And it is here that theologians and pastors most need each other. Theologians need pastors to make them aware of the situation in the church, and pastors need theologians to make them aware of what is new in the realm of ideas. At the same time, church members should not be surprised when theological students return with new ideas, for after all, that is why they study theology in the first place, to learn. One does not spend three to six years in advanced study and then preach and teach the same theology one had in Sunday school!

The task of the theologian is also hermeneutical, that is, one of interpretation.

> A theological system is supposed to satisfy two needs: the statement of the truth of the Christian message and the interpretation of this truth for every new generation. Theology moves back and forth between two poles, the eternal truth of its foundation and the temporal situation in which the eternal truth must be received.[16]

The theologian seeks truth on two levels, the eternal and the temporal. He or she deals with the texts of Scripture and the history and traditions of the church and then seeks to apply the truth which is uncovered to the contemporary cultural and historical situation. The theologian is, therefore, a bridge builder, seeking to span chasms between the past, the present, the eternal, and the temporal, the finite, and the infinite.

Most theologians, both those inside and outside of academia, spend a great deal of time in study and research. Often theologians are in the library or the study and are unavailable for other tasks such as preaching, speaking at conferences, and leading Bible studies. It should be kept in mind, however, that the theologian's contribution to the church is made with great care and concern. The theologian cares about truth and knows that "you will know the truth, and the truth will make you free" (John 8:32).

Real Persons and Abstract Principles

I began this inquiry with a consideration of humanity as the concern of theology, and I have concluded that the search for truth is the task of theology. This has not been accidental. The theologian is concerned both with persons (which includes the church) and with abstractions such as truth (which includes concepts of God). In all of this, however, the theologian keeps the person central. It is interesting to note this same emphasis in the doctrine of the Incarnation. Kosuke Koyama points out that even the finest doctrines are not the same as the real live person we meet every day, so that God chose not to send a doctrine about the person, but rather, to come as a man himself alive among us. "The best of all the good doctrines cannot compete with the one fact of God's incarnation in Jesus Christ."[17]

From the human Jesus we have moved to the cosmic Christ in our theological considerations, but if we look closely at the biblical record we find ourselves continually being drawn back to the real person. For the theologian, even the most abstract concepts and the most creative speculations always point back to the person, to the incarnation of God in Jesus Christ. In this we see that God, too, is a member of the caring community. The theologian as a caring person seeks to articulate and understand this mystery, and as a member of the human community, the believing community, the Christian community, and the learning community, seeks to meet the needs which arise from each of these diverse yet interrelated communities.

2

Doing Theology
in the Concrete

I have answered the question "What kind of person is the theologian?"
by suggesting that the theologian is a caring person responsible to at
least four segments of society—the human community, the believing
community, the Christian community, and the learning community. All
of this is somewhat abstract, however. How does one do theology in a
concrete situation?

One of the most concrete situations for doing theology, both from
a historical point of view and from a contemporary perspective, is
mainland China. Vast in size and cultural influence, China had considerable Christian influence during the sixteenth, nineteenth, and early
twentieth centuries. More recently, China has undergone thirty years of
no Christian influence to speak of. Yet the Christian church continued
to exist.

Now that restrictions have been lifted, the church is undergoing a
period of rapid growth. Many Christians in the West are wondering if
there may be a period of renewed missionary activity in China as well.
Numerous Christian organizations are publishing China newsletters,

and various mission executives have visited the country and returned to report on "the work" being done. One cannot help but appreciate this interest in China on the part of western Christians, and I believe that it is, for the most part, sincere.

China is, after all, one of the great unevangelized areas of the world. Anyone who takes Christian mission seriously must include China within the scope of that mission. The questions that face us, however, are: What kind of foreign Christian presence, if any, is appropriate to China today? How does one do theology in the concrete situation of contemporary China?

A Historical Perspective

In the past, several Christian missionary groups have penetrated China. The earliest of these were the Nestorians, who established a mission to China in A.D. 635 and built a church at Ch'ang-an in 638.[1] By the year 1000, however, Christianity was almost extinct. Although Nestorians returned to China in the twelfth and thirteenth centuries, when the Jesuits reached China in the sixteenth century "they found the very memory of Christianity there on the point of vanishing."[2]

This sixteenth century Jesuit mission to China was characterized by an openness toward Chinese culture and by greatly enlightened methods of mission. The period is synonymous with names like Matteo Ricci, Adam Schall, and Ferdinand Verbiest, three renowned Jesuit missionaries and scholars. They failed, however, due to the Chinese rites controversy (1628–1792).[3] The Jesuits allowed new Christian converts to continue observing certain Confucian rites honoring ancestors, understanding these rites to be an essential part of the Chinese culture and seeing in them no conflict with the Christian faith. Others in the church, however, took a different view. As the controversy intensified, decision making was shifted from China to Rome, until the missionaries and Chinese Christians were faced with a choice between submission to the Emperor in Peking or to the Pope in Rome. The Chinese would not tolerate outside influence in their affairs, and their attitude toward the Jesuits changed from acceptance to rejection. Persecution of the Christians followed, and the growth of the church was severely retarded.

The third great missionary penetration into China came in the nineteenth century and coincided with the expansion of western colonialism.[4] Literally thousands of foreigners—businessmen, missionaries, diplomats, tourists, and soldiers—flooded China. Their predominant motivations were financial gain and military conquest, and many missionaries found themselves siding with the westerners whenever conflicts arose. Gunboat diplomacy, unequal treaties, wars of aggression against China by foreign powers, and the internal breakdown of traditional Chinese society caught missionaries in the middle of one of the greatest social and political upheavals of all time. The twentieth century found China involved in a war with Japan on one front and a bitter civil war between Nationalists and Communists on the other front. With the birth of the People's Republic of China in 1949 the age of colonialism in China came to an end—and with it, the age of foreign missionary presence.

In the past, syncretism, foreign imperialism, and colonialism have crippled the Christian church in China and proved fatal to the foreign missionary enterprise. The reaction in contemporary China has been the Three-Self Movement—self-government, self-support, and self-propagation. For the past thirty years, the Christian church in China has been totally on its own with no foreign funds, controls, or influence whatsoever. What has emerged is a church that is totally Chinese and that is, after thirty years of isolation, apparently alive and well. While Christians in the West have been *calling for* indigenous and contextual theologies, the church in China has been *living* such a theology. Chinese Christians have had to struggle with their own cultural and historical context, and out of that struggle has developed a church that is once again looking outward toward the rest of the world. How then should the theologian as a caring person respond to this new openness?

Matteo Ricci as a Model for Doing Theology

It is obvious that there will be no sudden influx of foreign missionaries into China in the near future, if ever. Furthermore, any foreign presence will come about only at the invitation of the Chinese themselves. Gone forever are the days when one could "receive the call" and set out for China with little or no regard for the welcome that might or might not be waiting. Assuming, however, that the day comes when some foreigners will be welcome, we as Christians need to give serious consideration to the style of Christian presence that is most appropriate.

From the very beginning we need to be clear that the Christian mission *in* China is not synonymous with Christian foreign mission *to* China. There is a Christian church in China that has survived against overwhelming odds and has even grown in membership. Contrary to popular western opinion, the evangelization of China does not depend upon the West. Foreign missionaries may never be allowed to preach and solicit converts in present-day China. Evangelization in the traditional understanding of that term is a task for Chinese Christians, particularly those who have experienced the changes of the past thirty-five years. Only they are in a position to speak at this point in history. Christians in the West would do well to keep silent, listen, and learn.

It is highly probable that any foreign Christian presence in China will bear no resemblance to missionaries at all in the traditional sense. Foreign Christians in China may have formal ecclesiastical ties, but their primary relationship will be to educational and medical institutions, government agencies, and cultural and research organizations. They will be in support rather than leadership positions. At the same time they will be pioneers entering a new field of service; a field that is different geographically, politically, socially, and philosophically. Most significant of all, however, they will have to experience what Kosuke Koyama calls "the crucified mind."[5] In a very real sense they will find themselves doing theology in a situation not unlike that of Matteo Ricci in the sixteenth century.

For Ricci, preparation for a Christian presence in China began with nine years of study in Europe, three years in law and six years in philosophy and theology. This was followed by four more years of study, teaching, and exposure to different cultures in Goa, a Portugese colony in India.[6] Only after this initial preparation did he feel competent to begin his work in China. Upon arrival in China, Ricci assumed the role of a learner rather than a teacher. He began a serious study of the Chinese language, culture, history, and philosophy. Ricci had confidence in God's grace and refused to yield to the pressure of time for immediate results.[7] For him it was more important to be accepted by the Chinese on their terms than it was to make converts. He did not arrive in China with a fully developed program of action: "What distinguished his approach was rather an attitude of mind: respect for the people and culture of China, combined with unaffected humility which enabled him to adapt himself to his environment."[8] In a very real sense, Ricci went through an apprenticeship "during which he became deeply imbued with the Chinese point of view."[9] For Ricci, it was necessary to crucify the European mind and take on the Chinese mind.

It is significant that Ricci's work did not really get under way until this crucifixion of the mind had taken place. Ricci understood that Christianity would be accepted in China only if it adapted itself to what was best in Chinese civilization. He also realized that this adaptation would have to begin in himself, for "to do otherwise was unpardonable egoism."[10] As a result, Ricci avoided dependence upon the foreign mission structures in Macau as much as possible. He celebrated the Eucharist in private homes rather than in mission-built churches, and preferred to meet with the Chinese in small discussion groups following an evening meal. Ricci's presence was kept very low-key, for he understood that he was the guest and the Chinese were his hosts. It was not his place to go where he was not wanted, nor was he about to assert himself in a way that might offend his Chinese hosts.

In time Ricci accomplished a feat that has eluded most foreign missionaries to China; he was fully accepted as a member of the scholar-gentry class. "At last the China mission had a man who could stand before Chinese scholars, talk with them of scholarly things, and not be put to shame."[11] Not only was Ricci conversant in Chinese literature and philosophy, he was also able to read and write Chinese fluently. This latter qualification is most important, for the westerner in China who cannot read and write Chinese—no matter how fluent he or she is in the spoken language—is considered illiterate by scholars and consequently not accepted by them. Unlike a number of foreign mission boards in a hurry to make converts, Ricci was willing to take extra years to become fully literate in Chinese before he undertook his more overt mission activities.

Ricci's methods of mission have been summarized as follows:

1. study of language, culture and customs;
2. developing friendly contacts;

3. study of Chinese literary and philosophical classics;
4. wearing of Chinese styles in dress; and
5. alliance with progressive elements in Chinese scholarship.[12]

Following his arrival in Peking he developed this methodology further:

1. understanding the political system;
2. remaining convinced of the necessity for patience and prudence;
3. building a network of reliable contacts; and
4. continuing language study.[13]

It is significant that language study forms both the first and last points in Ricci's methodology. To be accepted by others on their terms is the essence of the crucified mind, and language study is perhaps the most difficult, and most important, element in this process.

Ricci also exhibited a rare ability to distinguish between that which is cultural and particular to a given time and place, and that which is universal and common to all people in all situations. Ricci was one of the first missionaries to take culture seriously. He was of the opinion that the Christian faith was universal, a viewpoint which reflected his sixteenth-century European background. At the same time, he understood that European culture was not universal, and in this he departed radically from the majority of Christian missionaries of his time. "He not only made an intelligent diagnosis of a totally unfamiliar condition, but he also, by implication, diagnosed *his own* condition and that of Western Christian civilization as a whole."[14] In confronting an alien culture and adapting Christianity to that culture, Ricci came to see that his own culture was only one of many cultures to which Christianity had become adapted. Christianity had adapted itself to Roman law and Greek philosophy; Ricci saw no reason why a similar adaptation could not be made to Chinese law and Confucian philosophy.[15]

This openness to the Chinese people and culture in no way weakened Ricci's Christian commitment. He was, after all, a missionary, and he did seek converts to the Christian faith. The Jesuit mission to China resulted in baptisms and the planting of a Christian church. Ricci's attitude of a crucified mind earned him a hearing among the Chinese, and they respected him and the Christian message he brought. This attitude, and Ricci's application of it, serves as a model for doing theology in China today.

Doing Theology in China Today

Ricci and the early Jesuit missionaries pointed the way to a cultural rapprochement and understanding between peoples of the world. They knew that "the problem of rapprochement between East and West is chiefly a psychological or spiritual one."[16] Furthermore, they were aware of the need for compromise. Syncretism—whereby one absorbs the other—and imperialism and colonialism—whereby one subdues or exploits the other—have clearly been rejected by the Christian church in China. During the past thirty years the Christian church has learned to compromise with the realities of China today. The government, in turn, has also compromised, and the church is once again allowed to function openly. Any foreign Christian presence in China is going to have to exhibit this same degree of compromise. The mission work of Matteo Ricci indicates how a foreign Christian presence in China might be undertaken should the opportunity arise. Ricci, as a caring person and as a theologian, demonstrated how to do theology in the concrete in China.

Perhaps the most significant aspect of a foreign Christian presence in China will be its effect not upon the Chinese, but upon Christians of the West. Ricci saw in China a new way of looking at his own culture and Christian faith. Contemporary Christians from the West who go to China will have the opportunity for this same experience. Says one observer of the current China scene: "I would propose that Christians would do well to test their life styles, social attitudes, and the social systems within which they live and witness by a broad and in-depth comparison with Chinese experience."[17] Western Christians should also test their theologies in light of Chinese experience. Much has been written in the West about the need for contextual theology. Christians in China know more about contextual theology than Christians in the West will ever know, for they have had more than thirty years of isolation in which to develop their own truly contextual theology. Western interaction with this theology may tell western Christians a great deal about themselves, and may even pass judgment upon certain aspects of western Christendom.

Ricci was willing to listen and learn from the Chinese. Christians in China today must be willing to do the same, for in so doing they will discover the relativity of their own position.

Christians may point to an absolute they see in the Christ experience, but our words will always be relative to our culture, class, ethnic background, and level of faith and understanding. It is our lack of self-awareness on this point, our inability to see our Christian formulations in all their relativity which caused many of our difficulties with China in the first place.[18]

The Christians of China have, in the last three decades, come to their own self-understanding. At this point in history both they and their government feel confident enough in that self-understanding to open the door once again to the outside world.

As Christians in the West consider how to respond to this new openness, a note of caution needs to be sounded. In all too many cases, the models being proposed for Christian presence and mission in China carry an air of triumphalism. Shortwave radio broadcasts are beamed into China with no regard for Chinese law. Bibles and Christian literature are smuggled into China in open defiance of the government. Groups are organizing with the idea of sending thousands of evangelists into China with no thought of first consulting the churches there. For all too many western Christians, the current openness of China toward religion in general and Christianity in particular is seen as the beginning of a great onslaught of missionaries, foreign funds, and unsolicited advice. Such a mission effort, if seriously attempted, cannot help but retard the Christian witness in China.

The Christian presence in China has already suffered three serious setbacks. If foreign Christians are given yet another opportunity to relate to China in a positive and supportive context, Matteo Ricci provides us with an example of how one might effectively do theology in the contemporary Chinese situation. Christians of China appear confident enough of their own self-identity to at least consider such a possibility. They know who they are. The question for Christians in the West is: do we know who we are? The form of any foreign Christian presence in China and the ways in which theology is done in that context will provide some answers to that vitally important question.

3

The Search for
a New Spirituality

An important but often neglected element in the theological enterprise is the formation, understanding, and practice of Christian spirituality. Asian Christians have been especially sensitive to spiritual concerns, due in part to the pluralism of religions in Asia. Although the Asian context is unique, the search for new forms of spirituality is found in religious communities throughout the world. Thus the search for new forms of spirituality in Asia can serve as a model for Christians in other contexts.

In 1975 the executive committee of the Association of Theological Schools in South East Asia voted to authorize among member institutions the search for a new spirituality rooted in the cultural and historical contexts of southeast Asia.[1] This concern for spirituality arose out of an evaluation of theological education in southeast Asia which concluded that education should be more than academic; it should involve a spiritual dimension as well.

In Asia as elsewhere, many laypersons in local churches believe that theologians and theological students are not concerned with the spiritual life. Academics and social concern are stressed in theological colleges, but few courses deal specifically with spirituality. As a result, theological students—and theologians too—are often unaware of their own spiritual heritage. With the rapid increase in secularization, many theological students feel uncomfortable with traditional forms of Christian spirituality such as praying before meals, daily devotions, and seminary chapel services. Many theologians show little interest in the spiritual disciplines such as fasting, prayer and meditation, and extended periods of solitude. Attention is focused on philosophical speculations in religion to the exclusion of the folk religious practices of the majority of people, until theological students and theologians are in danger of losing touch with an important area of their faith. Because this was causing anxiety in the Southeast Asian church, a search for a new spirituality was undertaken.

A similar concern is growing in the West, where secularization has reached a high point of influence and where academic theology and social ethics have long reigned supreme in the theological academy. New forms of spirituality—some drug induced, some rediscovered from the Christian past (eg. monasticism and communal or contemplative life styles), and some imported from Asia—give ample evidence that even highly secularized and technological societies experience a deep-seated need for the spiritual. It is significant that many people, including some Christians, are turning to Asia to fill this need. Thus it is vitally important that Asian Christians seek out and critically evaluate the spiritualities already present within the Asian context. Indeed, Thomas Merton has suggested that it is the responsibility of the Asian Christian to help save the spiritual heritage from destruction brought about by the influence of the West.[2]

The western experience has shown that there are grave dangers involved in exploring new dimensions of the spiritual life. It is no accident that in the Roman Catholic Church authentic mysticism has always been carried out within the wider framework of monastic orders and the authority of the Church. Protestantism, which lacks these built-in controls on spirituality, has until recent times remained skeptical concerning mysticism and other subjective spiritual experiences. Since drugs, illicit sex, various forms of mental disorders, involvement with the occult, and even experiences bordering on the demonic (as in the case of the Manson murders) can be associated with the spiritual life, the search for a new spirituality in Asia should definitely be undertaken within the framework of the church.[3] Spirituality must be theologically grounded and ecclesiastically controlled to avoid abuses. At the same time, spirituality is a part of and is conditioned by culture. Therefore it was fitting that the Association of Theological Schools in South East Asia become engaged in this search and attempt to focus on the specific spiritualities of southeast Asia.

Past Approaches in the Search
for a New Spirituality

The search for new forms of spirituality in Asia is not new, for a number of approaches have been taken toward spirituality in the past. All of these are, in my opinion, inadequate, but because each contains an element of truth, a brief historical survey will be helpful in setting the background for the current Asian search for a new spirituality.

One of the oldest Christian approaches to spirituality in Asia was that of the traditional missionary. Underlying this approach was the idea of religious or spiritual ethnocentrism: *we* are right and *they* are wrong, therefore it is *our* task to convert *them*. This view gave rise within the Christian tradition to such infamous activities as the crusades, the inquisition, and the use of gunboat diplomacy in China. One must, however, give traditional missionaries credit for their zeal, enthusiasm, and humanitarian efforts. Indeed, perhaps the positive element in the traditional missionary approach is the deep personal faith which motivated such efforts.

In spite of these positive aspects, negative aspects have tended to predominate. A Christian who holds to this approach will often have little feeling for differing cultural expressions of spirituality. Folk religions, temples with their liturgies and symbolism, monasticism, and religious philosophy will be seen as false, superstitious, even Satanic. A variety of this approach is to distinguish between natural spirituality and supernatural spirituality, with Christian spirituality being supernatural while that of the non-Christian is natural. This ethnocentricity and insensitivity has taught Asian Christians to reject their own native spiritual heritage. As a result, many Asian Christians are totally ignorant of the spiritual traditions of their own culture. Indeed, in Korea and Taiwan it is not at all uncommon to find Christians who have never been inside a Buddhist or Taoist temple and know nothing of non-Christian religions and spirituality. Surely the search for a new spirituality cannot be based upon the traditional missionary approach.

A second approach, the study of comparative religions, attempts to overcome the ethnocentricity of the traditional missionary approach by viewing non-Christian religions in relation to other forms of religion and spiritual life. Various spiritualities are compared and placed on a value scale, with tribal animistic religions at the bottom and the great world religions at the top. It should come as no surprise that many followers of this approach place Christianity at the top of the scale as the most highly developed religion in which God is most fully revealed. Unfortunately, some people who tend toward the traditional missionary approach have sought to give their views academic status by using the study of comparative religions as just another way of saying that we are right and they are wrong.

One cannot deny, however, that religions are different and that there are certain religious practices and beliefs which the majority of the world's people will reject as cruel, unjust, or intellectually and scientifically unsound. Value judgment is important when one seeks new forms of spirituality, and in this sense the study of comparative religions has something positive to offer. The difficulty is, one can easily overlook those practices and beliefs in Christianity which are cruel, unjust, or intellectually and scientifically unsound and assume that one's own spiritual tradition is the most enlightened and developed. Again one falls into ethnocentricity. For this reason many scholars in all parts of the world today prefer to approach non-Christian religions from the perspective of the history of religion or, as it is now often called, the science of religion.

The science of religion approach has attempted to correct the abuses of the study of comparative religions by seeking to be fully scientific and objective. Religion and spirituality are studied from a historical and phenomenological perspective, with no attempt to place various religions on a scale or to evaluate them. One only observes, describes, and understands religious behavior. The science of religion approach has done a great deal to enlarge our knowledge of humankind's religious and spiritual activity.

Unfortunately, by removing the element of value judgment, the science of religion approach has left many content to view religion and spirituality from a detached academic perspective. Yet the Christian, by virtue of his or her own faith experience and belief system, cannot accept a view of spirituality which takes no account of personal involvement. The subjective element is impossible to grasp through academic study alone. Thus the science of religion approach is, by itself, not acceptable to any Christian who speaks from the point of view of the believer. (This same subjective element is also present in various forms of non-Christian spirituality which the Christian may encounter.)

There are those today who assert that the great world religions are gradually fading out, that secular humanism is humanity finally come of age, and that spirituality is, in effect, a form of immature escapism from reality. According to this secularist view, humanity come of age must shed its religious beliefs and practices and assume full responsibility for its destiny. This view commonly takes two forms today—materialism in the West and Marxism in the East. This view, while it may contain elements of truth, is reductionist in that it attempts to view human spirituality from a purely scientific and rationalist perspective. The human person is a complex creature, and human inner spiritual needs cannot be so easily set aside. Following after Husserl and the phenomenologists, Dutch philosopher Herman Dooyeweerd has pointed out the significance of humankind's religious and spiritual roots.[4] The fact that in the secularized West new forms of spirituality are arising, and that in the Marxist East the important twentieth-century social critics (such as Pasternak and Solzhenitsyn) are, for the most part, deeply spiritual persons, cannot go unnoticed. Furthermore, in Asia, traditional religions are experiencing a rebirth and are far from dying out. Even folk religions are managing to thrive in such technologically developed countries as Korea, Japan, and Taiwan. Secularism alone cannot provide an adequate basis for the search for new forms of spirituality, for humanity is not only economic and political in orientation; it is spiritual as well.

At the same time, however, one must take into account the fact of secularism and what it means for the spiritual life. Secularism has given rise to a crisis of spirituality for modern humanity which has opened the door for new forms of spirituality to arise.[5] In addition secular forms of spirituality have appeared which pose both a challenge and an opportunity as Christians seek to speak to the needs of the modern world. While secularism cannot provide an adequate basis for the search for a new spirituality, it does provide new forms of spirituality which must be taken into account in any such search.

Another approach to spirituality is that of focusing one's attention upon doctrine. Here genuine openness may be desired, but is thwarted by an excessive concern with doctrine and rigid formulas of belief. The Christian may be so convinced of his or her doctrinal position that any dialogue with non-Christians is prejudiced from the outset. Even where this is not so, there is still the problem of doctrinal differences which are impossible to reconcile. This is particularly true concerning mysticism.[6] In spite of the fact that the mystical experience is present in all religions, many Christians—especially those of both orthodox and liberal activist persuasians—refuse to accept its reality upon a doctrinal basis. Thus there is no possible ground to appreciate mystical spirituality. In addition, stressing doctrine can lead to a complete turning away from the real-life spirituality of people, so that the focus of attention is shifted to what people believe. There can be no doubt that doctrine is a necessary element in religion and spirituality, but it alone cannot provide an adequate foundation for the search for new forms of spirituality.

A final approach to spirituality is absorbtion. This is especially important within the Chinese context, for the great religion of Buddhism which came to China from India was eventually absorbed into the overall religious and cultural framework of China.[7] According to Wen Yen Tsao, Confucianism in China was characterized by its tolerance of other points of view, fully realizing that these would eventually be absorbed into the general religious structure of China.[8] The result tended to be a syncretistic culture or folk religion. This can certainly be seen in Taiwan where there is a blending of Buddhism, Taoism, Confucian ethical thought, animism, and shamanism all together into one folk religion.[9] From the outset, mainstream Christianity has rejected this syncretistic approach, although not without a great deal of uncertainty—as witnessed by the Chinese rites controversy of the sixteenth century.[10] Today in China the Christian church remains a small but very distinct minority, having refused to become absorbed into the general religious system of China. On the other hand, the Christian church also tends to be isolated culturally from the intellectual and cultural life of the Chinese people. The question has been raised whether Christianity has become syncretized not with Chinese culture, but with western culture. In either event, syncretism has not resulted in any significant breakthroughs in the search for new forms of spirituality.

An Experiential Approach to Spirituality

I would suggest for all Christians a new approach toward spirituality, one which does justice to the major concerns of each of the above approaches yet avoids their pitfalls and opens up new possibilities. Specifically, I am speaking of the experiential approach.

The traditional missionary approach is concerned with particularism; an experiential approach safeguards and respects the Christian's personal experience and understands that such an experience might well be mediated through highly particular events and situations. Like the study of comparative religions, an experiential approach allows for value judgments concerning cultural forms of common religious behavior patterns. Like the science of religion approach, it looks at human behavior as it is and not as one would like it to be. It is based upon human experience—which is not only religious, but also secular. In addition, an experiential approach takes seriously the crisis in religion which is developing in largely secular environments. Doctrine is not ignored, for doctrine is understood as a way of explaining and organizing religious experience. Finally, while the experiential approach is not syncretistic, it does provide a foundation for dialogue and convergence of religions. There is even the possibility of a "central event in the history of religions . . . under which revelatory experiences are going on—an event which, therefore, makes possible a concrete theology that has universalistic significance."[11]

The experiential approach to spirituality has its philosophical roots in propositions concerning language stated by Ludwig Wittgenstein and other philosophers of language. "The common behavior of mankind is the system of reference by means of which we interpret an unknown language."[12] While this is obvious, it has often been overlooked; yet it is this which enables one to learn a foreign language and to communicate, perhaps by gestures and pointing, with a person who speaks an entirely different language. Religion has been compared to language by some theologians.[13] If we take Wittgenstein's idea and apply it to religion (the language of the spirit?) we can say that the common behavior patterns of humankind form the system of reference by which we interpret an unknown religion. Wittgenstein is careful to point out that "how words are understood is not told by words alone (Theology)."[14] Words, in and of themselves, are without meaning unless they refer to some concrete experience.

> These questions of compossibility, of potential actuality, are questions of the relations of concepts to experience; and consequently the radical question of meaning drives theological reflection beneath its own accustomed materials and authorities to the examination of ordinary experience. The purpose of such an inquiry is to find there those dimensions or regions of ordinary experience to which the language of religious symbols has reference, and so in terms of which such symbols can be said to have legitimate meaning and real possibility. This is for our age a new theological requirement posed by the radical questions with which we are faced in the contemporary situation of extreme secularity and radical doubt.[15]

Religious language, therefore, is not meaningful unless that language points toward religious experience. This is what Wittgenstein is saying when he points out that words are understood by more than words alone. He refers specifically to theology as an example.

In his *Asian Journal*, Thomas Merton points out that already those who work in the field of history of religions or science of religion have developed a form of religious language which is universal, in that it fits the religious experience of humankind even though that experience is expressed through vastly different cultures.[16] Thus the Christian, the Buddhist, the Hindu, and the Muslim can speak of personal religious experience in a meaningful linguistic frame of reference understood by those of other religious traditions. This is a forward step in the relationship between the religions of the world which will undoubtedly prove helpful in the search for new forms of spirituality within the Asian context.

At the same time, however, "every religious act, not only in organized religion, but also in the most intimate movement of the soul, is culturally formed."[17] Language itself is culturally formed, as is religion and its symbols. But these symbols "have their roots in the totality of human experience including local surroundings, in all their ramifications, both political and economic."[18] Thus religion has its roots in two levels of experience—that of the total human community and that of the more limited cultural community. I would suggest that the relationship between these two levels of experience is that of form and content. The basic common religious experiences of humankind are the content, while the cultural expressions of these religious experiences are the form. Culture, then, gives form to the basic content of human religious experience in much the same way that language gives form to the content of common behavior patterns. It is important to note, however, that either form or content by itself becomes an abstraction. Thus the meeting point between universal content and cultural form can play a significant and creative role in the search for new forms of spirituality.

In his last public lecture before his death, "The Significance of the History of Religions for the Systematic Theologian," Tillich spoke of this relationship between form and content:

> One must say that revelatory experiences are universally human. Religions are based upon something given to a man wherever he lives. He is given a revelation, a particular kind of experience which always implies saving powers. One never can separate revelation and salvation. There are revealing and saving powers in all religions. God has not left himself unwitnessed.[19]

According to Mircea Eliade, Tillich was radically reassessing his theological position, largely because of his visit to Japan, and was on the verge of beginning a new systematic theology based upon common human religious experiences rather than just upon the experiences of the Christian West.[20]

The experiential approach to spirituality seeks to focus upon universal content, but does so fully aware that content cannot be divorced from cultural forms. There is no "pure religion" free from all cultural influence and synthesis, just as there is no "true doctrine" which is not deeply rooted in religious experience. Even Barth, who in his earlier years was deeply opposed to the idea of religion, came to change his position in later years. "What is *Christian* is secretly but fundamentally identical with what is *universally human*. Nothing in true human nature can ever be alien or irrelevant to the Christian. . . ."[21]

An experiential approach to spirituality moves beyond the sharing of ideas, conceptual knowledge, and formulated doctrinal truth. "The kind of communication that is necessary on this deep level must also be 'communion' beyond the level of words, a communion in authentic experience, which is shared not only on a 'preverbal' level but also on a 'postverbal' level."[22] The framework for such an approach has been laid down by Kosuke Koyama in his book *Waterbuffalo Theology*. Here, speaking of Thai Buddhism, he makes a distinction between the study of Buddh*ism* and concern for the Buddh*ist*. According to Koyama, we study Buddh*ism*—the doctrine and the teachings—in order to more fully understand the Buddh*ist*—the person who experiences the fullness of life. Koyama does not say that the study of Buddh*ism* is not important, but he emphasizes that the -ism cannot experience life, only the -ist can do that. Furthermore, he points out that an exchange between Christianity and Buddh*ism* can often result in such an extreme defense of Christian doctrine that Christians cease to be Christ*ians* and become Christian*ity*. Of course, this also means that the Buddh*ist* is neglected and Buddh*ism* is brought to the fore. The significance of the experiential approach is that experience cannot be divorced from people. A Buddhist is first and foremost a person.

> When a man is a Buddhist, he does not cease to be a man. When a man is a Moslem, he does not cease to be a man. When a man is a Christian, he does not cease to be a man. A man does not cease to be 'man'. He does not become either an angel or a devil. By the grace of God, he remains man![23]

Indeed, Koyama asserts that if doctrine could satisfactorily explain man to himself, there would have been no need for the Incarnation.

I suggest, therefore, that the search for new forms of spirituality be based upon that in religion which is universally human—experience. At the same time, it must be thoroughly understood that this universally human experiential content takes on cultural form and therefore cannot be divorced from culture. Culture must be respected, cultural forms of religious experience appreciated and understood. As with language, the basis for communication between those of differing religious traditions lies in the content—their common religious experience.

Thomas Merton
An Experiential Understanding of Spirituality

Perhaps the best way to elucidate the experiential approach to spirituality is to cite an example of one whose entire life was dedicated to experiential spiritual understanding. Thomas Merton, a Roman Catholic monk of the Cistercian Order, spent twenty-seven years of his life—from 1941 until his death in 1968—as a member of the monastic community of Our Lady of Gethsemani Abbey near Louisville, Kentucky. Merton wrote close to seventy books and over three hundred articles dealing with the spiritual life, social criticism, war and racism, mystical theology, and eastern religions—especially Zen Buddhism. The last few years of his life were spent as a hermit in the hills several kilometers from the abbey. Although he rarely left the monastery grounds, Merton carried on a wide correspondence and had numerous visitors, including the French Neo-Thomist philosopher Jacques Maritain, the Chinese scholar John C. H. Wu, and the American political activist Daniel Berrigan. On one occasion, Merton was able to journey to New York City for several meetings with the Japanese Buddhist scholar D. T. Suzuki. Although a hermit, Merton kept in close contact with main currents of contemporary thought.

Fluent in several languages, Merton studied at Cambridge and Columbia Universities and spent a number of years at Gethsemani Abbey studying theology in preparation for ordination to the priesthood. However, he was much more than a scholar; he was also a deeply spiritual man. He was a man who knew Scripture and read the entire Psalter through each week. He was a man of discipline who rose at 2:30 every morning and closely followed monastic hours. He was a man of prayer and meditation, spending three hours every morning in predawn prayer. Merton was also a man who knew his own spiritual tradition—he knew the church fathers and was thoroughly familiar with the origin, history, and theology of Christian spirituality. Thus, when in his later life Merton turned his attention more and more to the spirituality of the East, he did so out of a deep personal knowledge and experience of his own Christian tradition.

Merton was a contemplative. He was a monk who knew mysticism from the depths of his own personal experience, and he experienced solitude as a hermit. When he began his search for new forms of spirituality, he naturally sought out those in the East who were also contemplatives and could share something of their experience with him. In 1968 a lifelong dream of Merton's was fulfilled: he journeyed to Asia to drink from the wells of Asian spiritual experience. He visited the Dalai Lama in India, met with hermits in Sri Lanka, and addressed interfaith groups of monks and nuns in both India and Thailand. Merton had planned to also visit Hong Kong, the Philippines, Taiwan, and Japan, but on December 10, 1968, he was electrocuted by a faulty electric fan at a Buddhist monastery on the outskirts of Bangkok.

Merton's life and work can serve as a model for us today as we seek new forms of spirituality in Asia. In his book *Mystics and Zen Masters,* Merton outlines what he considers to be the basis for interfaith spiritual understanding:

> Ecumenism seeks the inner and ultimate spiritual "ground" which underlies all articulated difference. A genuinely fruitful dialogue cannot be content with a polite diplomatic interest in other religions and their beliefs. It seeks a deeper level, on which religious traditions have always claimed to bear witness to a higher and more personal knowledge of God than that which is contained simply in exterior worship and formulated doctrine. . . . All religions, then, seek a "summit" of holiness, of experience, of inner transformation to which their believers—or an elite of believers—aspire because they hope, so to speak, to incarnate in their own lives the highest values in which they believe.[24]

Merton could take this position only because of his own experiences in the spiritual life. He was not a mere onlooker seeking out esoteric and exotic forms of spirituality, nor was he a rationalist theologian seeking to become more spiritual out of a sense of guilt. For Merton, spirituality was as much a part of his life as eating and drinking. Thus he found a natural point of connection—a meeting ground— with contemplatives in various Asian religious traditions. "One may find in all races and in all traditions both the capacity for contemplative experience and the fact of its realization even on a very pure level."[25] He continues, "While on the level of philosophical and doctrinal formulations there may be tremendous obstacles to meet, it is often possible to come to a very frank, simple, and totally satisfying understanding in comparing notes on the contemplative life, its disciplines, its vagaries, and its rewards."[26]

Merton, not blind to doctrinal differences, does point out that "there may still be great similarities and analogies in the realm of religious experience. . . . Cultural and doctrinal differences must remain, but they do not invalidate a very real quality of existential likeness."[27] He becomes quite specific on this point when he speaks of the difficulties in communication between the theologian and the mystic.

> Here again, the question is confused by the failure to distinguish between the objective theology of Christian experience and the actual psychologi-

cal facts of Christian mysticism in certain cases. And then one must ask, at what point do the abstract demands of theory take precedence over the psychological facts of experience? Or, to what extent does the theology of the theologian without experience claim to interpret correctly the "experienced theology" of the mystic who is perhaps not able to articulate the meaning of his experience in a satisfactory way?[28]

Commenting on D. T. Suzuki's study *Mysticism: Christian and Buddhist*, Merton points out that it was not Suzuki's intention to compare the mystical theology of Eckhart with the Buddhist philosophy of the Zen masters, but rather he was comparing "the *experience* of Eckhart, ontologically and psychologically, with the *experience* of the Zen masters. This is a reasonable enterprise, offering some small hope of interesting and valid results."[29] Thus Merton calls for an experiential approach to non-Christian forms of spirituality rather than one limited only to doctrine and theology.

Obviously, such an approach will raise doctrinal questions, especially concerning the subject-object relationship and the concept of God. But even here, Merton is open to new possibilities: as one looks a little deeper into the question of God "one finds that it is extremely complex and that the whole notion of *personality*, whether divine or human, will require considerable clarification before a real dialogue with the East can begin."[30] Such an openness can come only from experience, for rigid theological formulations generally would not even allow such a question to arise.

Spirituality is often criticized as being other-worldly, out of touch with vital social issues. Merton's books, articles, statements, and letters reveal a penetrating social concern coupled with insightful criticism of the evils of war, racism, and dehumanizing technology. "The way to find the real 'world' is not merely to measure and observe what is outside us, but to discover our own inner ground. For that is where the world is, first of all; in my deepest self."[31] Social action cannot arise from those who have nothing to give others but their own obsessions, ambitions, and ideas. True and meaningful social concern is discerning, loving, and peaceful in the fullest sense of those words. Social action results from being unified within one's self; therefore the fruits of inner contemplation will be concern for the social problems of the world. Drawing upon classical Chinese thought, Merton writes: "The way of Tao is to begin with the simple good with which one is endowed by the very fact of existence."[32] Merton often quoted Chinese sages. In speaking of the relationship between spirituality and social concern he wrote: "Chuang Tzu drily observed that the pursuit of the ethical Tao became illusory if one sought for others what was good for oneself without really knowing what was good for oneself."[33]

For Merton, spirituality could not be separated from everyday life, nor could spirituality be considered only from an abstract theological point of view. To know God meant to have an experience of God in one's own life. Thus "all forms of 'knowing,' especially in the religious sphere, and especially where God is concerned, are valid in proportion as they are a matter of experience and of intimate contact."[34] It was this kind of understanding which formed the basis for Thomas Merton's search for new forms of spirituality—a search which took him, finally, to Asia.

Some Remarks on Methodology

I have briefly introduced the need to search for new forms of spirituality in Asia and considered some major approaches used in the past in contact with non-Christian forms of spirituality. I have presented the experiential approach as a possible option for use in the present search and have cited the life and work of Thomas Merton as an example of how this approach has been put into practice. In conclusion, I offer six suggestions to anyone considering this experiential methodology:

First, know your own spiritual heritage, both intellectually and experientially. Your goal is not to study, but to encounter new forms of spirituality, and dialogue requires that both sides have something to offer. A Christian who does not know his or her own heritage and is not in vital contact with personal spiritual roots is not qualified to seek out new forms of non-Christian spirituality. Only a spiritual person can recognize and fully appreciate new forms of spirituality.

Second, begin not with those most different from yourself, but with those similar. Do not leap from mainstream Protestantism to Taoism or Buddhism, but first begin to appreciate forms of spirituality found within the Christian tradition—Roman Catholic monasticism, Protestant pentecostalism, Quaker quietism, Eastern Orthodox mysticism. Merton was not prepared to make his Asian journey until he had come to appreciate the spirituality of Southern Baptists!

Third, seek to know other non-Christian spiritualities and be open to changing your own position in light of what you learn. Be prepared intellectually before actual encounter takes place, for there is no excuse for ignorance. At the same time, personal experience is most important—spend a week or two at a Buddhist monastery or Hindu temple, visit area temples and shrines, observe funeral rites and festival days. Do not be afraid to ask questions. From this will come knowledge which may mean changing some of your own views about spirituality, both non-Christian and Christian.

Fourth, do not focus primarily upon doctrine, but rather upon common behavior patterns of religious and spiritual experiences. In this way you can reach a common ground which will provide a foundation for later doctrinal discussions. Focus on what is universally human— the content—then try to understand that content within the framework of this cultural form. The result will be a new appreciation of spiritual—and human—experience.

Fifth, openly face doctrinal problems and be willing to discuss them, but do not allow them to blind you to people and their experience, both human and spiritual. Doctrine is important, but people are more important. Christ came to redeem people, not doctrines. Even where doctrines are totally divergent, a striking similarity of experience may enable you to cross linguistic, cultural, and religious barriers.

Sixth, be willing to accept paradox and unanswered questions. Your encounter with other forms of spirituality will undoubtedly raise many questions, such as Merton's concept of personality in both its divine and human forms. Be open to these questions and be willing to accept the fact that answers may not be readily at hand. "There is no place for the cultivation of *one part* of human consciousness, *some aspect* of human experience, at the expense of the others, even on the pretext that what is cultivated is sacred and all the rest profane."[35] Spirituality is only one aspect of life, and we must beware of the danger of reductionism. The range of human experience is extremely complex. No one of us has all the answers to all of the questions. What is proposed here is only *a* methodology; it makes no claim to be *the* methodology. In the search for new forms of spirituality, feel free to live with unanswered questions and to experiment with a wide range of approaches and methodologies.

The experiential approach or methodology of which I speak seeks to encounter others at the deepest and innermost parts of their being.

> He who has understood the meaning of the dialogue will not want to have anything more to do with academic dalliance or a science of comparative religion, behaving as if it stood above all religions. He will also not want to know anything more of a certain kind of theology that works 'without presuppositions' and pleases itself in manipulating definitions and formulas and forgets about man, who is the main concern. He will be more and more pulled into what is called 'spirituality': the real life of the mind.[36]

Klostermaier tells of his visit with a Hindu who was famous for his opposition toward Christianity. After a two hour conversation, the Hindu, with tears in his eyes, told him: "If we insisted on our theologies—you as a Christian, I as a Hindu—we should be fighting each other. We have found one another because we probed more deeply, towards spirituality."[37] This is the spirit which should characterize our search for new forms of spirituality in Asia and throughout the world.

4

Theology as Grammar: Reflections on Theological Language

Language is one of the crowning achievements of the human race. Those of us who can use language in both spoken and written forms usually take it for granted, but if one must learn a new language in order to communicate, one soon acknowledges the importance of language. Those who cannot learn language skills are usually thought to be suffering from some kind of learning disability or mental or physical handicap. Those who have not learned to use language in its written form are referred to as preliterate or, if they live in a literate society, as illiterate, and great care is taken to see that their children are given the opportunity to read and write. The philosopher Ludwig Wittgenstein was correct when he wrote: "*The limits of my language* mean the limits of my world."[1]

This is nowhere more evident than in Asia with its many languages and dialects. I remember attending a meeting in Taiwan where eight languages and dialects were used in the course of a one-hour discussion. For this reason, many Asians are bilingual and even trilingual. In certain areas of Taiwan, for example, most people speak three languages—Mandarin Chinese, which is the national language; Taiwanese, which is the dialect of the island of Taiwan and Fukien Province; and Hakka, the local dialect where there is a concentration of Hakka Chinese. In addition, many older people speak Japanese, since they were educated during the Japanese occupation. If one lives in an area of Taiwan where all these languages are spoken, the size of one's world is in direct proportion to the number of languages one speaks.

A foreigner in such a situation soon discovers that his or her world is severely limited. A highly educated professor is reduced to infantile gesturing if he or she cannot speak at least one local language. In the Chinese context this limitation is exacerbated by the extreme difficulty in learning the written language, for it consists not of a phonetic alphabet but of literally thousands of symbolic characters which can be learned only through memorization. Failure to learn the written language reduces one to functional illiteracy in Chinese society even if one speaks several local languages. Language thus assumes extreme importance for the theologian living and working in a cross-cultural environment.

Ludwig Wittgenstein and Theological Language

One of the most creative approaches to the problem of language is found in the work of Austrian philosopher Ludwig Wittgenstein (1889–1951). Wittgenstein spent most of his life as a professor of philosophy in England, interspersed with periods of teaching school in his native Austria and living as a hermit in Norway. His major interests were mathematical philosophy and the philosophy of language. During his lifetime he published only one book, although a number of his manuscripts and notebooks have been published since. Wittgenstein's main concern with language was how we use it to communicate ideas.

Wittgenstein contended that we create language-games, and that in using a particular language we observe certain game rules in order to be understood. Thus the English have a language-game, the Germans have a language-game, the Chinese have a language-game, the Koreans have a language-game. Even dialects and various kinds of specialized language forms such as music, electrical engineering, medicine, and theology have unique vocabularies which will probably not be understood by those outside the particular discipline. Thus Wittgenstein emphasized that one must be certain which language-game he or she is playing. He also pointed out that "a language-game does change with time."[2] This means that words can have different meanings in different cultural and historical contexts. Therefore, two factors must be taken into account whenever we are using language to communicate: first, we must be certain that we are playing the same language-game, and second, we must be certain that we are playing the same variation of that language-game. Failure to take both of these factors into account will result in a possible breakdown of communication.

As a philosopher and logician, Wittgenstein was convinced that it is possible to use language in a clear and precise manner in order to communicate exactly what we mean. "Everything that can be thought at all can be thought clearly. Everything that can be put into words can be put clearly."[3] "A main source of our failure to understand is that we do not *command a clear view* of the use of our words."[4] This is nowhere more true than in our use of religious and theological language.

Although he was not in any sense of the word a theologian, Wittgenstein did say a great deal about the use of theological language. In his important *Philosophical Investigations,* published after his death, he wrote: "Grammar tells what kind of object anything is. (Theology as grammar)."[5] At first this seems like a rather puzzling statement, but further reflection shows that theology is by definition trying to say something about who God is and what God is like. The very word "theology" comes from the Greek *theos,* meaning "God," and *logos,* meaning in this context "discourse." Strictly speaking, therefore, theology is discourse or speaking about God: God-talk. God is the object of theology, and our grammatical statements about God attempt to communicate something of the reality of God. "Like everything metaphysical the harmony between thought and reality is to be found in the grammar of the language."[6] A word such as "Messiah" or "Savior" is a thought about the reality of God as seen in Jesus Christ; "it is in language that an expectation and its fulfillment make contact."[7] Indeed, language is the only way we can objectify our thoughts about metaphysical reality.

Difficulties with Theological Language

One of the difficulties with theological language is the problem of verification. "Reality is compared with propositions. A proposition can be true or false only in virtue of being a picture of reality."[8] Hence the statement "God exists" has no meaning if God in fact does not exist. A similar problem arises with almost any theological statement. Take, for example, the statement "Jesus Christ is my Savior." This immediately confronts us with the question of how closely this proposition corresponds to reality. If one seriously considers this statement, a number of questions arise: Who is the historical Jesus? What is the relationship between the Jesus of history and the Christ of faith? What is salvation? How can the life, death, and resurrection of someone who lived almost two thousand years ago save someone today? Is the resurrection an objective historical fact? If not, does this make a difference as far as salvation is concerned? These questions have profound implications for our language about God, Jesus, and salvation, for "If you are not certain of any fact, you cannot be certain of the meaning of your words either."[9] Much of the difficulty that exists in communicating the Christian message today can be explained by the uncertainty concerning statements of Christian doctrine. Such statements are not so much facts as they are beliefs, and therefore difficult to communicate with language alone.

A second difficulty which arises in the use of theological language is that of hermeneutics, or interpretation. "Our knowledge forms an enormous system. And only within this system has a particular bit the value we give it."[10] No single proposition or statement can be isolated from the whole. "What I hold fast to is not *one* proposition but a nest of propositions."[11] Therefore the proposition "Jesus Christ is my Savior" must be understood as part of a larger whole—a whole which includes propositions about God, the human person, sin, Christ, salvation, the church, and eschatology. The proposition "Jesus Christ is my Savior" is but one proposition in a whole nest of propositions known as Christian theology. When we invite someone to accept Jesus Christ as their Savior we would do well to remember that "When we first begin to *believe* anything, what we believe is not a single proposition, it is a whole system of propositions."[12]

This was dramatically illustrated by an event that took place several years ago in Miao-li, Taiwan. A well-known Christian evangelist held a gospel crusade at the local high school auditorium. Some months earlier, Billy Graham had held a large crusade in Taipei, and this evangelist was using some of Billy Graham's methods, including loud speakers to enable those outside the auditorium to hear. Several non-Christians sitting in front of their home several blocks away heard the service over the loud speakers, but had absolutely no understanding of what it was all about. Their comment was: "These Christians must be selling something. I wonder what they are selling?" The reason for their confusion was that in these non-Christians' system of propositions, one used a loud speaker system to attract customers to one's stall in the local market. Words like "Come to Jesus" and "Accept Christ as your Savior" led them to assume that the evangelist was trying to attract customers to his stall in order to sell a new product with the brand-name "Jesus" and "Christ." The evangelist operated out of one system of propositions, while the good folks sitting in front of their home operated out of entirely different and unrelated propositions.

The problem of interpretation takes on an added dimension when we realize that "only the accustomed context allows what is meant to come through clearly."[13] The Bible was originally written in Hebrew and Greek, Jesus spoke Aramaic, but today we read the Bible in English, Korean, Kouyü, Taiwanese, and a host of other dialects and languages. In each instance a transfer has been made from one language-game to another. Furthermore, great changes have taken place down through the years in each language-game, altering the meaning of many words and phrases.

The original Hebrew and Greek had no chapter and verse divisions. Yet all modern versions and translations of the Bible incorporate these divisions into the text. Furthermore, many modern translations also include paragraph divisions, but in an English Bible, a Korean Bible, and a Chinese Bible, the paragraph divisions are quite different. The accustomed context of each culture causes each to see the Bible differently and to group units of the text accordingly. Although the text itself is not changed, the way one perceives and understands that text may be greatly influenced. For this reason, many theological students are required to study Hebrew and Greek. Pastors and theologians need to get as close as possible to the accustomed context of the biblical writers.

The real difficulty with the accustomed context is not one of biblical translation, but rather of wrenching propositions out of their historical and cultural context and then expecting people to have a clear understanding of their meaning. In the statement "Jesus Christ is my Savior," the name "Christ" is immediately associated in most people's minds with the word "Christian." We tend to forget that Jesus was a Jew, not a Christian. We use the word "Christ" without thinking that the intended audience might not be aware that the correct terminology is not Jesus Christ but Jesus *the* Christ. Christ is in fact a title and as such it carries meaning within the Jewish context concerning the nationalistic aspirations of the ancient Jewish people, their concept of the Messiah, and the Jewish understanding of salvation. The word "Savior" really cannot be understood without some knowledge of ancient Jewish law and the sacrificial system which required a blood sacrifice for the atonement of one's sins. It would be extremely difficult for a person of the twentieth-century West to identify with anything remotely similar to the bloody sacrifices offered in the Jerusalem temple square, yet we continue to use theological language taken from that context.

In the Asian context, however,—Taiwan, for instance—animal sacrifices are still very much a part of the local folk religion. Salvation within the Jewish sacrificial context is a much easier concept to understand. In using theological language, we must bear in mind that Jesus spoke to his context using parables and that St. Paul did the same through Greek philosophy. In a similar manner, pastors and theologians today are called to speak to their own historical and cultural contexts. We would do well to ask anew what does the statement "Jesus Christ is my Savior" really mean? The answer to that question should then be stated in clear, understandable statements to the intended audience using the language-game of their accustomed context.

Human Behavior and Theological Understanding

Wittgenstein is careful to point out that there is considerably more to human understanding than mere words. "How words are understood is not told by words alone. (Theology)."[14] "The common behavior of mankind is the system of reference by means of which we interpret an unknown language."[15] In other words, all people, by virtue of their humanity, have certain common behavior patterns, and on the basis of these common behavior patterns we are able to learn another person's language-game.

This applies not only to national languages and regional dialects, but to the language-games of theology as well. Thus the statement "Jesus Christ is my Savior" implies a certain common behavior pattern found among all peoples in all situations—the quest for salvation. Salvation may be interpreted in many different ways, but the search for self-realization and a better life—a saving from things and conditions which keep us from fully realizing our human potential—is a common human behavior pattern. The key to communicating the statement "Jesus Christ is my Savior," therefore, is to find the same behavior pattern expressed in other historical and cultural contexts. Jesus spoke of sheep and a shepherd, St. Paul made use of Greek philosophy, and the writer of the Letter to the Hebrews drew upon Jewish law and tradition. The task of today's theologian is to discover behavior patterns of salvation as expressed today, not simply as they were expressed by biblical writers or Reformation theologians. To do anything less is to invite confusion about the meaning of our theological language.

Wittgenstein also alludes to another common behavior pattern which relates directly to theology. " 'You can't hear God speak to someone else, you can hear him only if you are being addressed'—That is a grammatical remark."[16] What he is referring to here is further explained in the final paragraphs of *Tractatus Logico-Philosophicus:* "There are, indeed, things that cannot be put into words. They *make themselves manifest*. They are what is mystical."[17]

In the realm of the mystical, however, we again encounter the problem of verification and must admit—at least philosophically—that no objective verification is possible. What verification does exist is personal and highly subjective, even though the mystical experiences are a common human behavior pattern. According to Wittgenstein, our language should concern itself only with those propositions that are clear, that correspond to reality, that take into account the total system of propositions and the accustomed context, and that communicate the intended meaning. In addition, our language should speak only of behavior patterns common to humankind. What then do we say concerning the mystical, when it cannot possibly include all of the above categories? "What we cannot speak about we must consign to silence."[18] It is here that we who use theological language on an almost daily basis make our greatest error. We do not know how to keep silent.

Let us write and speak only about what we know, making certain that our language is clear and that our intended meaning is communicated. Let us be certain that our theological statements and propositions correspond to reality and relate to the common behavior patterns of humankind. Beyond this, let us follow Wittgenstein's advice and keep silent.

5

Toward an Adequate Interpretation of Scripture

One of the crucial tasks for a Christian theologian is to develop adequate principles for interpreting Scripture, for the biblical text is one of the foundation stones upon which theology is built. In the West, biblical interpretation, or hermeneutics, has reached such a level of sophistication that it has become almost a separate discipline from either biblical studies or systematic theology. In Asia therefore, a number of people are suspicious of the principles of biblical interpretation because they believe that hermeneutics is a western discipline alien to Asian thought forms. In all too many instances the Christian message has been presented in western thought forms using western philosophical categories. If one task of biblical interpretation is to present the message of Scripture to coincide with the proclamation of the church in Asia, then an adequate method for interpreting Scripture within the Asian context must be developed.

The Past and Present in Asian Hermeneutics

While hermeneutics is a western science in that its name derives from Greek and its major philosophical influences and theological developments have come from Germany, the practice of textual interpretation is as old as religion itself. Ancient civilizations believed that sacred texts must be kept pure from corruption. Furthermore, divergent readings and interpretations had to be resolved. In the New Testament, the Pharisees, the Saducees, and the Samaritans all have differing principles of biblical interpretation. Textual interpretation, then, is by no means a western development.

Textual interpretation has been important for all the ancient religious and philosophical traditions of Asia. "What has been learned for the maintenance of true religion has been carried out as a literary discipline, and textual criticism is one of the oldest of intellectual studies."[1]

The *I Ching* or *Book of Changes* is one of the oldest Chinese philosophical texts and books of divination. The text itself is not particularly long, but literally thousands of commentaries have been written on the *I Ching*. The *Tao Te Ching,* attributed to Lao Tzu, is only about five hundred characters in the original Chinese. Yet it, too, has given rise to commentaries numbering in the thousands. In many instances the commentaries and interpretations have been read more than the original texts themselves. Throughout Chinese history controversies have raged between "old text" and "new text" schools of thought, each expending great effort to demonstrate that one's own particular school has the most authentic text.

Textual criticism and interpretation was highly developed in Chinese Buddhism by Buddhist missionaries who came to China from India. As early as A.D. 400 they used a method known as "matching the meaning" whereby Taoist texts were used as a source for words and phrases to convey Buddhist meanings in the translations of the sutras into Chinese.[2] This same method was also used as a teaching device, so that unfamiliar Buddhist concepts were introduced through Taoist thought forms. It was said of one student of Buddhism, Chu Fa-ya: "Each time he, together with Tao-an and Fa-t'ai, unravelled the knots of perplexity and resolved doubts, they jointly exhausted the essential purport of the scriptures."³ Between A.D. 360 and 434, Buddhist teachers and scholars emphasized understanding the meaning that lay beyond the words of a text. "The purpose of symbols is to gain a complete understanding of ideas, but once the ideas have been gained, the symbols may be forgotten. The purpose of words is to explain the truth, but once truth has been uttered, words may be dispensed with."⁴ An illustration often used was that of a fisherman using a bamboo trap to catch fish. Once the fish are caught, the fish trap is forgotten, for it served only as a means of catching the fish. Thus early Buddhists in China followed well-developed principles of textual interpretation.

Various schools of Confucian philosophy had their own principles of textual interpretation, and the interpretation of Confucian texts has varied greatly during the last two thousand years. Different dynasties followed different principles of interpretation. In the Han Dynasty (206 B.C.–A.D. 220) most scholars tended to interpret Confucian texts from a literal, factual, and historical perspective. The Neo-Confucianists, represented by the philosopher Chu-hsi (1130–1200), looked at the same texts from a more philosophical and subjective point of view. They emphasized practice over mere recitation. Confucian scholars in the Ch'ing Dynasty (1644–1912) revolted against both the literalism of the Han and the subjectivism of the Sung by coming up with their own principle of interpretation, practical experience.⁵

A similar development of textual interpretation can be found in other Asian countries such as Korea, Japan, and India, and hermeneutical insights of the Asians are often strikingly similar to those of twentieth-century interpreters of Scripture. A Confucian hermeneutic, for example, followed three basic interpretations of Confucian texts: the literal and factual; the experiential; and a combination of the first two with an emphasis upon knowledge and action. Realizing that such a comparison is by no means exact, it is nevertheless interesting to compare Confucian hermeneutics with recent biblical scholarship, which has developed three major schools of thought: the historical-critical method, interested in historical facts; the existentialist method, concerned with action and personal experience; and the so-called new hermeneutic, which seeks to combine the best of the other two into a method that stresses both historical facts and personal experience. Aside from the fact that the Chinese were chronologically ahead of the

West in textual interpretation, East and West have tended, in this instance, to think along similar lines. Perhaps the fundamental difference is that current western biblical interpretation brings two new elements to the Asian experience: the scientific method and a philosophy informed by a rigorous logic, both of which were absent in ancient China and other Asian civilizations.

Christianity in China has also been through several stages of development, each characterized by unique hermeneutical principles based upon available knowledge and missionary attitudes. (It should not be necessary to point out that some of these attitudes have not furthered the acceptance of the Christian message by the Chinese.) The earliest Christians to arrive in China, the Nestorians, were gradually absorbed into the general religious system of China until they completely lost their identity by becoming part of local religious practice and belief. Nestorians are now all but forgotten except for such archaeological remains as the famed Nestorian inscription. The majority of Christian missionaries who later came to China—with the notable exception of the Jesuits in the sixteenth century—sought to impose western practices, theologies, and church divisions upon the Chinese, with the result that Christianity today is a small, dedicated minority quite marginal in terms of overall influence.

About twenty-five to thirty years ago, the situation in other Asian countries was much like that in China. Asian Christians became increasingly dissatisfied that Christianity was so western in its orientation and began to develop a new theological perspective known as indigenous theology. The basic principle was that each country would develop its own theology, based upon its own cultural heritage. The result, at least in China, has been a highly individualistic, spiritualized, and fundamental piety characterized by an emphasis upon the laity, spiritual experiences, and a literal interpretation of Scripture. Theology in the formal academic sense has been rejected in favor of group Bible study. In some cases, a strong anti-foreign bias totally rejected any foreign influence whatsoever. The teachings of Watchman Nee are one example of such an indigenous theology; it is found in Taiwan in such churches as the True Jesus Church and the Little Flock. While indigenous theology has resulted in a strong sense of personal piety and commitment, it has exhibited little theological depth and almost no social concern. In effect, indigenous theology has so centered on the culture that it has isolated itself from outside influences, thus cutting itself off from the world church.

As a result of these weaknesses of indigenous theology, the current trend in Asia has been a movement toward contextual theology. Like indigenous theology, contextual theology sees the culture as the context in which theology is developed and applied, speaks to the issues of each context, and seeks to do theology from the philosophical and cultural foundations of that context. However, contextual theology also seeks to establish a theological depth that can be critical of the culture. As a methodology, contextual theology does not reject outright all that is western, nor isolate itself from contacts with the worldwide church, yet it tries to avoid the pitfalls of excessive westernization. Contextual theology thus attempts to provide a better method than either the isolationism of indigenous theology or the westernism of the traditional missionary approach.

Perhaps the greatest difference between indigenous theology and contextual theology lies in their long-range goals. Indigenous theology originally was an attempt to indigenize western theology into non-western contexts. This accounts for the fact that much indigenous theology is simply fundamentalism transplanted from the West into an Asian context. Contextual theology, on the other hand, seeks to actually develop new theologies from the cultural contexts at hand. The result has been an enormous surge in theological creativity.[6]

A basic assumption of contextual theology is that a synthesis of Christian theology with various culturally-based philosophies and religious practices is both practicable and desirable. If western Christianity can borrow from Hebrew tradition, Greek philosophy, Roman law, and German and French existentialism, then why cannot eastern Christianity borrow from Confucianism, Buddhism, Taoism, and other Asian philosophical and religious systems? Cannot God speak through Asian cultural contexts as well as through European and American contexts?

There are, however, several issues which arise at this point. First of all one can, as does the Dutch Christian philosopher Herman Dooyeweerd, question the whole validity of synthesis theology. According to Dooyeweerd and his followers, what is needed is a uniquely Christian philosophy upon which to construct Christian theology.[7] While this may be a worthy ambition, Dooyeweerd has not shown how such a Christian philosophy can avoid the problem of being culturally conditioned. A second issue is how the identity of the Christian faith can be maintained in the non-Christian context. What is essentially Christian and what is cultural? The dividing line between these two is often very fine, which can cause serious problems in developing a contextual theology. A third issue is whether it is realistic to expect people from such ancient cultural areas as China, India, and Japan to turn to Christianity in any great numbers. Americans and Europeans are very resistant to new religious movements coming in from Asia; why should not Asians feel the same way about Christianity coming into their own cultural environment? Contextual theology is greatly needed, but it is by no means certain that it will make any appreciable difference in terms of the growth of Christianity in an alien and even hostile cultural setting.

Asia is an area, however, where much serious and creative theological work remains to be done. Developments in biblical interpretation taking place in Asia today have arisen out of a background of indigenous and contextual theology. Biblical scholars and theologians are now developing principles of biblical interpretation out of their historical and cultural contexts. Three such principles of biblical interpretation are Kazoh Kitamori's theology of the pain of God, Kosuke Koyama's water buffalo theology, and Emerito Nacpil's Critical Asian Principle. These are by no means exhaustive. I could mention the third-eye theology of C. S. Song, the homeland theology of Wang Hsien-chih, the minjung theology of Korea, and numerous other Asian theologies that have developed guiding principles for biblical interpretation. I have selected these three because they were among the formative contextual theologies of Asia, and they have had considerable influence upon biblical interpretation.

Kazoh Kitamori
Theology of the Pain of God

Kazoh Kitamori's book *Theology of the Pain of God* was one of the first contextual theologies from Asia to appear in English.[8] It was published in Japanese in 1946 soon after the end of World War II. The Japanese nation had suffered a humiliating defeat, they were now occupied by American troops, and their industrial plants and cities were in ruins. In addition, the Japanese had suffered the terrible effects of two atomic bombs and were uncertain about future effects of radiation. Most significantly, the Japanese culture had been shaken to its very roots—the emperor was, by his own admission, not divine; for the first time many long-standing traditions were being called into question. For the Japanese people, this was truly a time of great pain. Kitamori's book sought to speak theologically both from and to this particular context.

"Dr. Kitamori's fundamental concern is, of course, to re-root the gospel of Christ for the Japanese mind."[9] At this particular point in history it was imperative that the Christian gospel speak to Japanese pain if it was to be meaningful at all to the Japanese mind. Thus Kitamori writes:

> My prayer night and day is that the gospel of love rooted in the pain of God may become real to all men. All human emptiness will be filled if this gospel is known to every creature, since the answer to every human problem lies in the gospel. Therefore I pray "May thou, O Lord, make known to all men thy love rooted in the pain of God." The greatest joy and thanksgiving comes from the knowledge that this prayer is being granted and that step by step this gospel is becoming real to mankind.[10]

Kitamori brings two Japanese words, *tsutsumu* and *tsurasa*, together and, using Jeremiah 31:20 and Isaiah 63:15, constructs the basis for his theology of the pain of God. *Tsutsumu* means to enfold or to enwrap and *tsurasa* means to feel pain in one's deep personal self for the sake of others. Thus he constructed a concept of vicarious suffering which refrains from revealing how deeply one suffers and keeps pain within oneself for the happiness of others. In Jeremiah 31:20 the Hebrew reads "my bowels are troubled." Isaiah 63:15 expresses a similar Hebrew concept: "the sounding of thy bowels and of thy tender mercies." In both instances these words refer to the suffering and pain of God toward his people. Says Kitamori: "Ever since this strange word struck me, I have meditated on it night and day."[11] Kitamori, through his idea of the pain of God, came to see human pain Christologically. Whenever one person suffers for the sake of another, that person analogically participates with the suffering of Christ on the cross. " 'Love rooted in the pain of God' cannot be observed objectively outside of

our human experience. There is no way to see it other than experiencing
it in our own life."[12]

Kitamori's book was written in 1946 when the pain of the Japanese
people was most acute. In 1958, in the preface to the fifth edition, he
states: "I myself do not find the necessity of using the 'pain of God' as
a theological term any longer, since this term has served its purpose
adequately in stressing the mediatory and intercessory love of God over
against the immediate love of God."[13] As the situation of the Japanese
people changed, as they recovered from the devastation of the war, and
as their pain became less acute, the theological term 'pain of God'
became less intense in its meaning. Kitamori then sought to develop his
theology in a direction which would speak more to the current context
of the Japanese people. Thus Kitamori demonstrates contextual theology at work not only in terms of the Japanese culture, but also in terms
of that culture at a particular historical period. The context for theology
and biblical interpretation has not only a cultural dimension but a temporal dimension as well. Kitamori's hermeneutic attempted to do justice
to both of these elements.

Kosuke Koyama
Water Buffalo Theology

Kosuke Koyama, a student of Kitamori's, is a Japanese theologian
who for a number of years taught in a theological seminary in Thailand.
Later he served as Dean of the South East Asia Graduate School of
Theology with offices in Singapore, then taught for several years at the
University of Otago in New Zealand before joining the faculty of Union
Theological Seminary in New York. This rich theological experience
within a number of different cultures is reflected in his numerous writings.[14] In his best-known work, *Waterbuffalo Theology*, he sets forth his
basic theological method. The very title of the book is suggestive of
Koyama's theological and hermeneutical approach, while the chapter
divisions clearly demonstrate that it is an exercise in biblical interpretation: Part I, Interpretation of History; Part II, Rooting the Gospel;
Part III, Interpretation of Thai Buddhist Life; and Part IV, Interpretation of the Christian Life. Koyama begins by dealing with the unique
historical situations in Asia generally and then with each nation spe-

cifically. He speaks of the Asian cyclical view of time, the Asian experience of colonialism, and the Asian reaction to technology. After laying this foundation, Koyama then speaks of the need to re-root the Christian faith in Asian soil. Asia, because of its unique cultural and historical context, has theological problems which demand approaches and methodologies that fit its own needs.

Because he was a theological education missionary sent from Japan to Thailand, Koyama is well qualified to speak in detail concerning problems of re-rooting the Christian faith into the soil of Buddhist Thailand. He asserts that this process of re-rooting the Christian faith will demand from the missionary a new interpretation of his or her own Christian faith and new insights concerning denominationalism, the concept of personality, the uniqueness of Asian urban life, and the need for the missionary to have a crucified mind.

One especially creative aspect of Koyama's theology is his vivid imagery. Beginning with a brief passage of Scripture, Koyama then relates it to some aspect of Asian life. Chapter titles include: "Will the Monsoon Rain Make God Wet? An Ascending Spiral View of History," "Gun and Ointment," "Aristotelian Pepper and Buddhist Salt," and Cool *Arahant* and Hot God."

Koyama's vivid imagery comes directly from his experience of living and working in Asia.

> On my way to the country church, I never fail to see a herd of water buffaloes grazing in the muddy paddy field. This sight is an inspiring moment for me. Why? Because it reminds me that the people to whom I am to bring the gospel of Christ spend most of their time with these water buffaloes in the rice field. The water buffaloes tell me that I must preach to these farmers in the simplest sentence–structure and thought–development. They remind me to discard all abstract ideas, and to use exclusively objects that are immediately tangible.[15]

Koyama is emphatic that the Christian message must be presented in terms which the people (in this case the farmers of Thailand) can identify with and understand. He places the needs of the farmers over the theologies of Aquinas, Barth, and others, and uses vivid images rather than abstract ideas to communicate the gospel.

Koyama bases his approach to theology upon Scripture, citing I Corinthians 9:22–23; "To the weak I became weak, that I might win the weak. I have become all things to all men, that I might by all means save some. I do it all for the sake of the gospel, that I may share in its blessings." He also asserts that it is his task to "read the Scriptures and theological works with *your* [Thai rice farmers'] needs in mind."[16] For Koyama Scripture and the great theological works of Aquinas, Calvin, and Barth accomplish nothing unless they can be interpreted and clearly understood. This means that

> the theology for northern Thailand begins and grows in northern Thailand, and nowhere else. Northern Thailand theology, the theology that serves Jesus Christ in northern Thailand, will surely come into being when we dare to make this decision. In this decision is the beginning of a theology for Thailand and for Asia.[17]

It is important to point out that Koyama is not opposed to systematic theology; he just wants to use theology to interpret the Christian message to those who do not think in abstract categories.

Koyama also asserts that the major concern for the theologian should not be religion or culture, but rather, the people who practice a religion and live in a culture. Thus one studies another religion and/or culture not just for its own sake, but to better understand the people of that religion and culture.

> As my relationship with Buddhist friends increased and my language comprehension grew, I came to realize that what really matters is not a set of doctrines called Buddhism, but *people* who live according to the doctrine of the Buddha, or I should say who are trying to live according to the doctrine of the Buddha. Accordingly, my interest shifted from Buddhism to Buddhist people.[18]

Koyama points out that Buddhism does not suffer, does not sweat, does not get hungry, and does not desire material possessions. A Buddhist, however, does all of these things, because he is a human being. Thus Koyama emphasizes the Buddh*ist* and not Buddh*ism*.

Several principles of biblical interpretation can be discerned in Koyama's basic theological methodology:

1. His hermeneutic, like the Christian gospel, is concerned for people and not for theological ideas or systems.
2. Academic theology, while necessary for a pastor and theological teacher, is always read with a clear understanding that it will be interpreted in the context of the people with whom one is work-

ing. The usefulness of theology is determined by the extent to which it can benefit those people.

3. Interpretation begins not only where the interpreter is, but with the particular situation of those for whom the interpretation is being given, for each person is unique. Thus Koyama makes use of simple, vivid images common to the daily life of the Thai people. (One is reminded that Jesus did not speak in theological terms, but rather in parables, vivid stories of things common to his hearers' daily life.)

4. Koyama's hermeneutics requires the interpreter—be it missionary, pastor, or theologian—to be emptied of his or her own presuppositions in order to understand the presuppositions of the people for whom the interpretation is being made. Koyama refers to this as "the crucified mind." In a sense, the interpreter is called upon to become a personal incarnation so the gospel message can be communicated with meaning and power.

5. Involvement with a given culture is the only soil in which theology germinates. Culture forms the general context for theological reflections, and includes customs, language, social behavior, and thought patterns. Thus all theology is contextual theology. Even as St. Paul uses Hebrew tradition to minister to Jews and Greek philosophy to minister to Gentiles, so the contemporary interpreter must use northern Thai images and traditions to minister to the people of northern Thailand.

6. Theology is biblically based. East and West may differ in terms of philosophy, theology, and traditions, but all Christians use the same Bible. In Scripture we find a universal source for theological insight, practical instruction, and devotional inspiration. Contextual theology, therefore, is rooted not only in culture and history, but also in Scripture.

Emerito Nacpil
The Critical Asian Principle

Emerito Nacpil, a Philippine theologian and churchman, served as president of Union Theological Seminary in Manila and Dean of the South East Asia Graduate School of Theology before becoming a

Methodist Bishop in Manila. During his tenure as Dean of the South East Asia Graduate School of Theology, he travelled widely throughout Asia and the world; thus he brings to his theological thinking a wealth of cross-cultural experience. Nacpil's unique contribution to hermeneutics and biblical interpretation has been the development of what is called the Critical Asian Principle.

As a specific concept, the Critical Asian Principle had its beginning at a meeting of the senate of the South East Asia Graduate School of Theology in Bangkok in 1972. The Graduate School, a consortium of schools in southeast Asia, was developing a doctoral program in theology, and desired that the orientation of the degree program should be distinctly Asian. When the doctoral program was approved, Nacpil suggested that this Asian orientation be applied not only to the doctoral program, but to all programs of the South East Asia Graduate School of Theology. From then on the Critical Asian Principle became important for the whole task of theology and mission carried out by the church in southeast Asia. As Dean of the Graduate School at that time and one of the region's leading theologians, Nacpil was instrumental in applying the Critical Asian Principle to theological education and continuing development of the concept.

As currently applied, the Critical Asian Principle "seeks to identify what is distinctively Asian, and use this distinctiveness as a critical principle of judgment on matters dealing with the life and mission of the Christian community, theology, and theological education, in Asia."[19] In a brief essay Nacpil sets forth seven characteristics of Asia as a distinct region in which to do theology:

1. Asia has a plurality and diversity of races, peoples, cultures, social institutions, religions, and ideologies.
2. Most of the countries have had a colonial experience.
3. Most of the countries are in the process of nation-building, development, and modernization.
4. The peoples of this region want to achieve authentic self-identity and cultural integrity in the context of the modern world.
5. Asia is home of some of the world's great living religions, and these have shaped the culture and consciousness of most

Asians, thus representing alternative ways of life and experience of reality.

6. Asian peoples are in search of a form of social order beyond the current alternatives. They are looking for a form of social order which would enable them and humankind to live together in dignity in a planetary world.

7. The Christian community is a minority in the vast Asian complex.[20]

The Critical Asian Principle is an attempt to use these seven characteristics as the basis for doing theology in the Asian context.

In the same essay Nacpil cites four ways in which the Critical Asian Principle may be applied. In summary these are:

1. As a *situational* principle whereby theology is done within the varieties and dynamics of Asian realities.

2. As a *hermeneutical* principle suggesting that the gospel and Christian tradition are understood in the light of those Asian realities, interpreted in relation to the needs and issues of the Asian situation, and that Asian realities are understood in light of the gospel and its tradition.

3. As a *missiological* principle which seeks to develop a missionary theology that will illumine Asian realities in the light of the gospel and help to direct changes in the regions along lines consonant with the gospel and its vision for human life in God.

4. As an *educational* principle which gives shape, content, direction, and criteria to theological education in southeast Asia.[21]

Although one could certainly call the Critical Asian Principle an overall hermeneutical approach, Nacpil has chosen to emphasize that it is a hermeneutical principle by which biblical interpretation in Asia can be guided. Undoubtedly the Critical Asian Principle is a cornerstone of the emerging theology of Asia.

There are, of course, numerous other theologians in Asia who are making significant contributions to biblical interpretation and contextual theology. Kitamori, Koyama, and Nacpil are only three examples of the creative theological work currently being carried out within the Asian context. The search for an adequate interpretation of Scripture underscores the importance of Scripture for the theological enterprise in Asia. Perhaps the day will not be long in coming when hermeneutics will have come full circle, when we in the West will gain new insights from Scripture and the Christian tradition because of theological work done by our brothers and sisters in Asia.

6

Culture, Philosophy, and Church Unity

Cultural values and the philosophical concepts which undergird such values play an extremely significant role in Asian churches. In different cultures, differences are vast even among churches of the same denomination. In Korea, for example, the majority of Protestants are Presbyterians, yet Presbyterians in Korea are divided into at least four major denominations and approximately thirty smaller groups. In Taiwan, the majority of Protestants are also Presbyterians, but there is only one major Presbyterian denomination with three or four very small groups. What factors cause such a great difference in church life? What is the role of culture and philosophy in the life and work of the church? I shall examine these questions as they relate to church unity in the Presbyterian Church in Taiwan.

The Quest for Church Unity

Anyone familiar with Presbyterian-Reformed tradition knows that church unity among Presbyterians is most elusive. In the United States alone there are at least twenty-one distinct Presbyterian-Reformed bodies.[1] These divisions are due to a number of factors. Several of these churches are ethnic in origin; the Reformed Church in America and the Christian Reformed Church are largely Dutch, while other bodies have their roots in Germany or Scotland. Some churches, such as the former Presbyterian Church in the United States (now reunited with the United Presbyterian Church in the U.S.A. to form the Presbyterian Church, U.S.A.), came into being as a result of the Civil War. Still others, such as the Orthodox Presbyterian Church and the Bible Presbyterian Church, arose because of disputes over theology. One of the most recent Presbyterian groups, the Presbyterian Church in America, formed as the result of a combination of social, political, and theological factors. Regrettably, as these bodies have sent missionaries to other countries, they have exported these divisions as well.

The Presbyterian Church in Taiwan is unique in that it has maintained its unity for well over one hundred years. Today there is only one major Presbyterian-Reformed body in Taiwan—the Presbyterian Church in Taiwan. There have been minor splits and defections, usually involving two or three congregations, but most of these have been due to influences such as politics or foreign missionaries who bring their own divisions to Taiwan. Interestingly enough, even when missionaries bring in extremely conservative theology, those holding to that theology usually do not leave the church. For the most part the Presbyterian Church has maintained a unity that baffles observers from other countries. This is not to say that the Presbyterian Church in Taiwan has not had ample grounds for division, both from within and without. The church is divided ethnically and linguistically, so that on any Sunday morning worship services are conducted in thirteen languages and dialects. Various political issues, such as the declaration of human rights, create great controversy, as does the continued existence of the North Synod after the South Synod dissolved itself into the General Assembly. And, as in all Presbyterian-Reformed churches, theological differences have arisen over the nature and authority of Scripture, the virgin birth of Christ, and other issues. Yet while many foreign groups have tried to take advantage of opportunities for division, and people like Carl McIntire have made repeated trips to Taiwan, the Presbyterian Church in Taiwan has been able to achieve that elusive goal, church unity.

The Presbyterians of Taiwan are, of course, sinners like the rest of us. There *are* divisions in the Presbyterian Church in Taiwan, as attendance at any presbytery meeting will clearly demonstrate. Sometimes these divisions have run so deep that, on occasion, presbyteries have split. One example was the so-called Spirit Movement in several mountain presbyteries. This charismatic movement caused such deep divisions that a group broke away from one presbytery. This break-away group did not leave the Presbyterian Church in Taiwan, however. The dispute was strictly an "in-house" matter eventually resolved so that the presbytery reunited. Divisions caused by power politics within the church, disputes over control of property and institutions, even theological issues have not caused factions to leave the denomination and start a new one. Presbyterians in Taiwan, like Presbyterians everywhere, are no strangers to controversy; unlike many other Presbyterians, however, they tend to keep their disagreements within the family.

The Presbyterian Church in Taiwan is, therefore, a rather unusual phenomenon within the Presbyterian-Reformed tradition. It is an ethnically divided church with a membership which reflects a high degree of political and theological pluralism. It is a church that has had more than its share of disputes and that seems, on the surface at least, to be ripe for division. Yet, in the midst of all this, it is a church that cherishes its unity. Why? What makes the Presbyterian Church in Taiwan different? How is this church unity maintained?

The Maintenance of Church Unity

A clue to the unity of the Presbyterian Church in Taiwan can be found in a visit which I made to a local pastor's study. There on the wall were banners and plaques from various organizations with which the pastor and the church had been associated. Three items immediately stood out—a banner from the Billy Graham Crusade, a plaque from the Nora Lam Crusade, and an honorary degree from Faith Theological Seminary bearing the signature of Carl McIntire. To the western mind, blending Billy Graham's evangelism, Nora Lam's charismatic faith healing, and Carl McIntire's fundamentalism would be both unthinkable and impossible. Such differing views would be mutually exclusive categories. Indeed, many Presbyterians in the West, of both conservative and liberal persuasions, would find all three viewpoints incompatible with their understanding of Reformed theology.[2] What makes all of this even more interesting is that the Presbyterian Church in Taiwan is a member of the World Council of Churches and very actively involved in a number of controversial political issues. At the outset, therefore, we see a tendency toward synthesis coupled with a corresponding lack of concern for the law of contradiction.

Another clue can be discerned in occasional rumblings heard among Presbyterians of Taiwan about the "new theology" being taught in seminaries. In the United States, such concerns have caused professors to lose their positions and new seminaries to be founded.[3] In Taiwan, however, neither of these has happened. The only new seminaries in Taiwan have been founded and funded by foreigners and overseas Chinese. There have been no great controversies over the inerrancy of Scripture, nor have any professors been tried for heresy in church courts. Rather, when such concerns arise they are dealt with quickly, quietly, and generally fairly and honestly, and they never reach the General Assembly level. A tendency toward discretion and compromise can be seen, a "both/and" mentality in contrast to the western "either/or."[4] In short, the Presbyterian Church in Taiwan has refused to be drawn into various theological squabbles that have characterized many other Presbyterian-Reformed bodies.

Some people have attributed Taiwan's church unity to the depth of spiritual life found among Taiwan's Presbyterian community. On the surface, however, Korean Presbyterians seem more devout—as evidenced by early morning prayer meetings, prayer mountain retreat houses, and churches with membership in the tens of thousands. Yet the Presbyterian churches in Korea are divided into over thirty distinct groups.[5] Others have suggested that the Presbyterian Church in Taiwan derives its unity from its creedal position—but the twenty-one American Presbyterian churches are also creedal in their doctrinal bases. Still others are of the opinion that the Presbyterian Church in Taiwan is unified by its Taiwanese ethnic identity, yet out of a total of 962 congregations in 1979, 436 were mountain churches where the Taiwanese language was not used. It would appear, therefore, that we must look elsewhere for the basis upon which this church unity is maintained.

I believe that unity in the Presbyterian Church of Taiwan is not so much theological as it is cultural and philosophical. The island of Taiwan is, of course, culturally Chinese in that its various ethnic groups have all been influenced by what has been called classical Chinese culture.[6] Basic social mores, the family structure, the political system, and the philosophical framework have all come from China. To be sure, they have taken on a unique Taiwanese form, but just as Americans look to Europe for their cultural roots, so the people of Taiwan look to China.[7]

Culture has been defined as "the socially shared mental content" of a people; as such, it exists only in the form of ideas.[8] People of varying cultural traditions share common ideas about social mores, family structure, politics, and philosophy. Traditionally a great deal of effort has gone into understanding *what* people of different cultures think; only recently has the emphasis shifted to *how* they think and how they formulate ideas and beliefs.[9] I believe that the key to understanding how the unity of the Presbyterian Church in Taiwan is maintained lies in understanding how the people of Taiwan formulate their ideas and beliefs.

I have already mentioned their tendency toward the synthesis of what, to the western mind, appear to be contradictory points of view.

> The tendency to combine different and even opposing elements into a synthetic whole is characteristic of Chinese thought. We will recall that, with Lao Tzu, *Tao* is conceived as both "is" and "is not," a point further developed by Chuang Tzu, to become his famous theory of the equality of things. We will also recall that Confucius held the Mean to be the highest ideal, to the rejection of anything one-sided or extreme. We will recall, too, that in Neo-Moism the distinction of substance and predicates, of the universal and the particular, etc., was severely criticized. The Yin-Yang tradition was, through and through, a tradition of synthesis of opposites. The whole movement of medieval Chinese philosophy was not only a continuation of the central emphasis on synthesis of the ancient schools, but was itself a synthesis of the opposing philosophies of Confucianism and Taoism. This synthetic tendency, which affected practically all indigenous Chinese philosophies, also affected Buddhism in China.[10]

It is significant to note that Buddhism was a foreign religion introduced into China from India, and that all of the various schools and sects of Buddhism came to China, yet only those able to adapt to the Chinese way of thinking lasted.[11] Christianity has also been influenced by this tendency toward synthesis, as can be seen by the Taiwanese pastor who includes Billy Graham, Nora Lam, and Carl McIntire into the scope of his ministry. The Presbyterian Church in Taiwan is, by virtue of its Chinese philosophical heritage, predisposed toward inclusiveness rather than exclusiveness, toward synthesis rather than division.

This idea has been developed theologically by the Korean theologian Jung Young Lee. Lee contrasts the eastern way of thinking— "both/and"—with the western way of thinking—"either/or."[12] Asians can hold two opposite statements together in creative tension; western thinkers, on the other hand, consider the law of contradiction one of the essentials of logical thought. This makes it difficult if not impossible for a westerner to hold two contradictory positions at the same time. The Presbyterian Church in Taiwan, however, has no difficulty in doing so, much to the consternation of western missionaries and other observers. While this may lead to a seeming laxity concerning pure doctrine, it also leads to an ethnically, politically, socially, and theologically plural church. The Presbyterian Church in Taiwan includes theological conservatives and liberals, mountain people and plains people, rich and poor, charismatics and social activists, and political reactionaries and radicals. While American Presbyterians tend to divide along these lines in an "either/or" fashion, the Presbyterian Church in Taiwan maintains its unity by thinking in terms of "both/and."

Chinese thought is also characterized by its holistic style. While westerners tend to divide, categorize, and analyze, the Chinese think in terms of the whole. From a western point of view, this kind of thinking seems imprecise—indeed, almost inarticulate, because knowledge of this kind is generally expressed in paradoxes, images, and symbols.

> The fact is that Chinese philosophers were accustomed to express themselves in the form of aphorisms, apothegms, or allusions, and illustrations. . . . Aphorisms, allusions, and illustrations are thus not articulate enough. Their insufficiency in articulateness is compensated for, however, by their suggestiveness. The more an expression is articulate, the less it is suggestive—just as the more an expression is prosaic, the less it is poetic. The sayings and writings of the Chinese philosophers are so inarticulate that their suggestiveness is almost boundless.[13]

Indeed, the very structure of the Chinese language is concise but very imprecise. A single character may suggest any number of meanings, and most great philosophical works written in Chinese are of less than one hundred pages. In spite of this, literally thousands of pages of commentaries have been written on these works, and they continue to suggest new interpretations in every age.

We find, therefore, that Chinese Christians have not produced much in the way of classical systematic theology. Rather, their theological writings have been limited to essays or short works on specific issues, symbols, or themes. Rather than analyzing a particular concept—salvation, for example—the Chinese theologian will select a particular image which is suggestive of salvation and then give it a number of different interpretations.[14] The theology which results is suggestive rather than exhaustive, interpretive rather than definitive. Where western theology tends to have a certain finality about it—can anything more be said after Barth's *Church Dogmatics* or Rahner's *Theological Investigations?*—Chinese theology tends to be a theology in process which draws the reader into a never-ending course of interpretation.

This unique method of doing theology has practical implications for church unity in that it rejects the idea that there is only one true interpretation of a given text, including the biblical text. Hajime Nakamura traces this methodology back to Buddhism:

> In the Chinese Buddhist tradition there is no single authoritative interpretation of a given phrase. Chinese Buddhist scholars produced different and varied interpretations of the same phrase. Rather than compel a uniform belief they interpreted phrases very freely. Zen Buddhism carried this to extremes enunciating the principle "not to set up any words." Similarly, "if our mind goes astray we are ruled by the *Lotus-Sutra*. If our mind is enlightened, we rule the *Lotus-Sutra*." "Not to set up any words" does not mean "do not resort to the use of the written words,". . . . The term . . . means, rather, "do not set up dogmas in the form of propositions."[15]

This method of doing theology has had two important consequences for the unity of the Presbyterian Church in Taiwan. First, most Presbyterian theologians and biblical scholars have rejected the propositional view of biblical revelation. God is too imprecise to be reduced to propositions in a book. The Presbyterian Church in Taiwan has, therefore, avoided the rigid biblicism that has divided the Presbyterian-Reformed churches elsewhere. Secondly, Taiwanese Presbyterians are quite tolerant of theological diversity. Since many interpretations are possible, it follows that no one interpretation should become authoritative. This understanding of theological pluralism strengthens church unity, for it sees theological doctrines as only a means and not an end.

The Presbyterian Church in Taiwan is further reflective of Chinese culture in that people take precedence over ideas. Theological doctrine has no intrinsic value; rather, its value is determined to the extent that it contributes to the happiness and well-being of humanity. If theological disputes become so fierce that they divide people, then a compromise must somehow be found so that relationships are restored. This is an example of the Mean or Middle Way. Thus when seminary professors are accused of teaching "new theology," the affair is not blown up into a major confrontation between the conservatives and the liberals, for such a confrontation would divide the church and place doctrine above people. The Presbyterian Church in Taiwan prefers to quietly work out a compromise whereby no one loses face: the professor retains his teaching position, the critics have their faith in the seminary restored, and the conservatives and liberals can continue working and worshipping together. In all of this, the unity of the church is maintained.

The unity of the Presbyterian Church in Taiwan, therefore, is based in large part upon modes of thinking derived from its Chinese philosophical heritage. This philosophical heritage influences the theology of Taiwan as well as the practical affairs of church life, even though most Presbyterians of Taiwan are probably unaware of these underlying philosophical assumptions. Sometimes the most important assumptions are those of which we are unaware.

The Preservation of Church Unity

The Presbyterian Church in Taiwan is in no sense an isolated church. It has fraternal relations with churches throughout Asia, North America, and Europe. Numerous missionaries from these churches serve in Taiwan, and many of them teach on the faculties of Taiwan's theological schools. At the same time, an increasing number of advanced theological students from Taiwan are studying abroad, particularly in North America and Europe, and many pastors are travelling to Korea and the United States for church growth seminars and mission studies. In the course of this internationalization of theological and mission education, the Taiwan church is being exposed to western theology and to Asian adaptations of western theology, particularly in Korea and Japan. Always present, but not always obvious, are western philosophical assumptions and categories of thought. What effect will this have upon the unity of the church in Taiwan?

Taiwan is fortunate in that its western colonial experience was limited to a few short years. Furthermore, Taiwanese theologians have never been attracted to German theology to the same extent as theologians in Korea and Japan. Of all areas of Asia, Taiwan is perhaps in the best position to seek its own way theologically and to root its theological life and work in its own Chinese philosophical worldview rather than one imported from the West. Indeed, Taiwan's unique cultural and historical situation may give rise to new interpretations of old philosophical presuppositions, thus stimulating the rise of new ways of doing theology.

The problem facing the church in Taiwan today is that of philosophical—and therefore cultural—integrity. It is vitally important that the Chinese philosophical heritage be preserved if the unity of the church is to be preserved, for church unity almost certainly cannot be built upon western philosophical presuppositions.[16] It is important that Chinese philosophical thought be included in the curricula of theological schools, for theological students need to be taught to appreciate their own philosophical heritage and to think creatively in it. This does not mean, of course, that western philosophy and theology should be excluded from the theological curriculum, but that they should always be taught from a critical perspective. Eastern and western philosophies and theologies should interact with the clear understanding that in Asia one does theology within the Asian context.

Foreigners working with the church in Taiwan need to become aware that they bring with them underlying assumptions of western philosophy—the law of contradiction and its "either/or" manner of thinking. The western tendency for abstraction and analysis and inclination toward precise use of philosophical and theological terms will result theologically in an emphasis upon systematic thinking, propositional statements of doctrine, and the view that one doctrine or theological position is correct and therefore authoritative. Westerners working in the Chinese context must develop a self-awareness of their own unconscious philosophical assumptions.

> Half of today's Christendom lies outside the fenced cloisters of traditional theology. . . . Thus the Church has become kerygmatically universal, but is still theologically provincial, in spite of the great giants of theology. This is a serious dilemma, and if we do not resolve it, it will destroy our foundations as the Church in the world.[17]

In short, we in the West must realize that our theology too, is contextual, for "the most fundamental differences among the 'worlds' with which the Christian communicates are the differences among the *philosophical* 'worlds.' "[18]

As the Presbyterian Church in Taiwan faces the future, two areas must be considered to preserve the unity of the church. First, the church must look to its own cultural heritage and philosophical roots to guide its life and work. Second, westerners who relate to the Presbyterian Church in Taiwan need to become familiar with the Chinese cultural and philosophical heritage and at the same time be sensitive to western philosophical presuppositions which they might unknowingly impose on others.

Christians from the West may discover great significance in Presbyterian unity in Taiwan—something that may be needed to bring about the unity we seek but cannot attain. It may well be that the key to our own Christian unity lies not in the councils of the West, but in the churches of the East—in churches such as the Presbyterian Church in Taiwan.

7

Theological Method: Four Contemporary Models

Contemporary theological construction has tended to focus on four basic methodologies: classical systematic theology, philosophical theology, political theology, and contextual theology.[1] Western theologians have generally favored the first two methodologies while Third World theologians have focused on the latter two. This chapter examines these four methods of doing theology and four theologians who model them, and discusses how each offers strengths for doing theology in Asia today.

Taiwan, because of its unique historical situation, has been influenced by all four of these methods of theological construction. British and Canadian missionaries who arrived in Taiwan over a century ago brought with them classical Reformed theology. This was systematic theology at its best—comprehensive, logical, rational, and highly organized. The influence of systematic theology in Taiwan continued for roughly the next ninety years, climaxing with the influence of the theology of Karl Barth in the 1960s and even into the early 1970s. Even today, the Presbyterian Church in Taiwan has been characterized by outside observers as being largely Barthian in its theological stance, although this probably only once again reflects the Chinese tendency to take the middle way—in this case, between theological conservatism and liberalism.

Beginning in the 1950s an interest arose in philosophical theology as well. From the conservative side came names such as Gordon Clark, D. Elton Trueblood, and Cornelius Van Til.[2] In the Netherlands a new Christian philosophy appeared, associated with Herman Dooyeweerd and D. H. Th. Vollenhoven.[3] At the same time, thinkers representing a more critical theological position began to raise questions concerning religious language, the existence of God, and the possibility of miracles. Especially significant was the publication of a collection of papers in 1955 entitled *New Essays in Philosophical Theology.*[4] Theological schools, including those in Taiwan, responded by adding courses in apologetics and philosophy of religion. The basic approach of Taiwan seminaries, however, continued to be western with an emphasis upon Aristotelian categories and rationalism.

In the 1960s and 1970s, rising theologians in Asia such as Shoki Coe, Kosuke Koyama, Choan-Seng Song, and Emerito Nacpil began to focus their attention on the unique historical and cultural contexts of Asia. In what has come to be known as contextual theology, new appreciation was expressed toward traditional religions, non-western ways of doing philosophy, and various lifestyles unique to the many cultural groups in Asia. Theology was not only re-rooted in Asian soil, but an attempt was made to develop entirely new theologies that grew directly from that soil.

Theology took yet another turn in the mid-1970s when political considerations came more and more to the fore. Questions concerning human dignity, social justice, economic opportunity, and participation in the political process increasingly became the concern of theologians—in Taiwan as elsewhere. At times contextual theology and political theology were quite distinct; more often than not, however, they were blended together into a creative synthesis of theory and praxis.[5]

Looking to the future, I cannot help but speculate about where theology will be going. Are there methodologies on the horizon that offer hope for new theological construction? If so, where are they, and what relationship, if any, do they have with the four methodologies I consider here?

Four Contemporary Theological Methods

Systematic theology, generally speaking, is concerned first with the dogmatic task—setting forth the Christian faith as found in Scripture and expounded in the creeds and confessions of the Christian church. Systematic theology emphasizes doctrine and rational belief. Second, it deals with a certain content that has been revealed in Scripture and with the revelation of God as recorded in Scripture. Hence, revelation is an important element. Third, the dogmatic task is never carried out individually or in isolation; systematic theology is understood to be a function of the organized church and is done in the service of the church. Finally, systematic theology is by definition systematic and structured. Traditionally there have been six loci for systematic theology: the doctrine of God (theology proper), the doctrine of the human person (anthropology), the doctrine of Christ (Christology), the doctrine of salvation (soteriology), the doctrine of the church (ecclesiology), and the doctrine of the last things (eschatology). Most systematic theologies will be arranged in this order or will at least deal with all six areas. Systematic theology, then, is comprehensive and universal in its perspective.

Philosophical theology is first of all concerned with the apologetic task—interpreting the Christian faith to the contemporary world in meaningful, understandable terms. The philosophical system provides a foundation upon which the theological system is constructed, explained, and defended. Second, philosophical theology is rational in orientation, seeking to answer questions and reduce mystery. It desires to achieve both clarity and consistency of thought, and to explain the unknown or the difficult satisfactorily. Third, because philosophy is used in all theological construction—hopefully intentionally but more often than not unintentionally—philosophical theology seeks to consciously decide not *whether* to use philosophy in theological construction, but rather, *which* philosophy to use. Finally, philosophical theology, like philosophy itself, is concerned with the following areas: ontology (the nature of being), cosmology (the nature of origins and process), epistemology (the nature of knowledge), aesthetics (the nature of form and beauty), and ethics (the nature of good and evil). Thus philosophical theology tends to be problem-oriented and seeks answers to questions posed in each of these areas.

Political theology has as its primary concern the ethical task—effecting change in society so that one's theology is lived out in the world. It emphasizes practice over theory, focusing not upon constructing theological systems but upon actually *doing* theology. It is characterized by an emphasis upon social and communal structures rather than upon individual and personal faith. In addition, political theology is not limited to ecclesiastical structures, but seeks to work within existing social and political structures to bring about change. In many cases political theologians actually join the struggle to change the existing social and political order. Political theology tends to understand the Kingdom of God not in terms of a future eschaton, but rather as a realized eschatology in the here and now. Metaphysical speculations are avoided in favor of concrete human and social realities. Finally, the material and physical needs of humanity are stressed as equally important as spiritual needs; the whole person is the focal point of political theology.

Contextual theology is concerned with the hermeneutical task—the interpretation of the Christian faith in cross-cultural situations. It seeks to be both faithful to the text and relevant to the context. Contextual theology is characterized first by a serious consideration of culture as the matrix of theology and what this means for one's total worldview and way of thinking—metatheology in the fullest sense of the word. Second, it is generally biblical in emphasis, so that much of the actual theologizing consists in pointing out relationships between the biblical worldview and the worldviews of non-western cultures. (Of course the same process operates in terms of western cultures: strictly speaking they, too, are contextual theologies.) Third, contextual theology makes a conscious attempt to re-root the Christian faith into each unique culture and restate Christian theology in the philosophical categories and thought forms of each culture. Finally, it stresses the particular as opposed to the universal—expressing what God means in a given historical and cultural context as opposed to speaking generally about such universal categories as creation, sin, redemption, or eschatology.

Systematic theology and philosophical theology have a long and honorable history in western theological thinking. Political theology, traditionally carried out by those of the anabaptist and peace church traditions, has in some of its more recent forms taken on an increasingly radical stance and has thus posed a direct threat to traditional theology and church life—especially in areas of ethical and social concern. Contextual theology is the most recent of the four methods under consideration. For the first time, non-western philosophical categories are finding their way into theological discourse, which poses a direct challenge to traditional western theology. Taken together, these four methodologies comprise distinctly different ways of doing theology, yet each has something to offer the contemporary student of theology and the contemporary church.

Four Models for Doing Theology

Theologians who represent each of these four theological methods model what it means to do theology today. The theologians I shall consider have certain characteristics in common: each is still living and active theologically; all have carried on a lively interaction with other contemporary theologians and are thoroughly acquainted with dominant theological trends of the day; each has written a short book setting forth his methodology in language understandable to both the specialist and non-specialist; each is considered a leading thinker in contemporary theology; and each is an articulate and respected spokesperson for his particular model of Protestant theology.

Systematic Theology

The last of the really great systematic theologians in the Reformed tradition and probably in all of Protestantism is G. C. Berkouwer (b. 1903) of the Theological Faculty of the Free University of Amsterdam in the Netherlands. Although he retired from teaching in 1970, he remains active theologically and continues to work on his *Studies in Dogmatics* which have now reached fourteen volumes.[6] Unlike many European theologians, Berkouwer did not have a crisis of faith in which he broke from liberalism. Rather, he has always represented the more evangelical wing of the Reformed Church. Yet his theology is appreciated by conservatives and liberals alike for its fairness and thoroughness. Throughout his career Berkouwer has carried on a lively debate with Barth and with leading representatives of the Catholic tradition.[7] This latter concern led to his being invited to be an official observer at

Vatican Council II. His earlier books tended to be somewhat polemical, but in later years he has mellowed to the point where some of his more conservative colleagues have expressed doubts concerning his orthodoxy. A thorough reading of Berkouwer provides one with a solid background in Reformed theology written from the perspective of the systematic theology model.

Berkouwer's theology is centered around the principle of co-relation, which asserts that theology is in constant and dynamic relationship with faith and therefore with the Word of God on one hand, and with the church and the pulpit on the other.[8] To be relevant, theology must live and work at the center of this double polarity. Theology itself is a work of faith, hence the believer must be able to recognize theological statements as objects of faith. The purpose of theology for Berkouwer is not to construct a logically coherent system as such, but rather to creatively respond to the Word of God. Theology is therefore biblically based and natural theology is rejected. However, even though theology is based on revelation, the Incarnation does not exhaust revelation; God's revelation in Christ does not negate other revelation.

Theology for Berkouwer is definitely carried out in the service of the church. Theology is done on a confessional basis, yet creeds are not absolutized. Creeds are never the terminal point for theological discussion, but a point of orientation for doing theology. Furthermore, theology should not say new things simply because they are new. The task of the theologian is not to propose new dogma, but to understand the truth of God in each new situation. In addition, theology must be preachable; it must be able to reach the person in the pew. Because Berkouwer's theology tends to avoid abstractions, it is a rich source of sermon material for the pastor.

Finally, Berkouwer's theology involves confrontation with differing points of view. Throughout his career Berkouwer has continually been in dialogue with opposing points of view, most notably those of Barth and the Catholic tradition. However, he has always confronted others in a spirit of love and has made it a point to criticize his opponents not at their weakest point but at their strongest point. It is this characteristic that has given Berkouwer's theology such a wide audience in the contemporary church.

Philosophical Theology

One of the leading forms of philosophical theology on the contemporary scene is process theology, largely based on the work of philosophers Alfred North Whitehead and Charles Hartshorne. Process theology is a uniquely American model for doing theology. The leading theologian of this school is John B. Cobb, Jr. (b. 1927), a Methodist who teaches at the Claremont School of Theology in California. Along with David Ray Griffin (b. 1939), who also teaches at Claremont, he has founded the Center for Process Studies and has written widely in the area of process thought. Cobb is the author, editor, and co-editor of a number of books, and has written well over one hundred articles. He is probably one of the best-known American theologians working today. However, because he is a philosophical theologian, his work is not well known to the average church member. Most recently Cobb has become involved in a fruitful dialogue with scientists in the biological and ecological fields and with non-Christians, particularly Buddhists in Japan.[9]

Cobb's theology is best explained in two books, *Process Theology: An Introductory Exposition* which he co-authored with Griffin, and a collection of essays edited by Griffin and Thomas J. J. Altizer entitled *John Cobb's Theology in Process*.[10] Cobb contends that an integral Christian theology that is truly contemporary must assume responsibility for a critical investigation of both the Christian tradition and the modern world vision. Thus Cobb asserts that historical consciousness must inform our understanding of the distinctive character of both the central Christian vision and the central visions of modern and postmodern traditions. It is Cobb's opinion that this critical investigation of the cognitive claims of Christianity and modernity can best be carried out when philosophy is the principal conversation for theology. For Cobb the philosophy of Alfred North Whitehead is best suited for this task.

Cobb's theological method can be summed up as follows: first, contemporary Christian theology must employ the methods of historical and cultural analysis to clearly show the distinctive "visions of reality," "structures of existence," and "cognitive beliefs" of both Christianity and modernity; second, theology—operating on the logic of commitments to meaningfulness and truth operative in both the Christian and modern positions—must also make use of philosophical criteria; finally, the findings of this process may require a new formulation of the central theistic belief of classical Christianity. Cobb is empirical in his approach, even to the point of suggesting that we may need a new Christianity.

The process theology of Cobb and his followers is a conscious attempt to construct a theology based upon a contemporary philosophical system. Unlike systematic theology, process theology is open-ended, bound neither by Scripture nor by the creeds and confessions of the church. Proceeding on the assumption that the philosophy of Whitehead is the correct one for doing philosophical theology, process theologians seek to integrate the Christian faith into the process vision of reality.

Political Theology

Almost certainly the best known political theology on the contemporary scene is liberation theology. Largely developed by Latin American theologians, liberation theology is now finding spokespersons throughout the Third World and even in the developed nations of the West. One of the most articulate liberation theologians writing today is Robert McAfee Brown (b. 1920), a Presbyterian living and working in the United States. Brown has had a varied career involving teaching, administration, and ecumenical affairs. He has taught at Union Theological Seminary in New York, Stanford University, and is currently at Pacific School of Religion in Berkeley, California. Brown considers himself as being in theology *and* ethics, for he understands these two disciplines as being necessarily related to each other. Consequently his theological work has been characterized by controversy due to his involvement in social and political affairs and Third World concerns. His book *Theology in a New Key: Responding to Liberation Themes* is perhaps the best available introduction to liberation theology, particularly as this theology is found in Latin America.[11]

Six distinctive methodological perspectives set liberation theology apart from both systematic and philosophical theology. First, the starting point for liberation theology is the poor. This assumes that the world should not be the way it is and that poverty has causes that can be corrected. Second, the dialogue partner for liberation theology is not the non-believer, but the non-person. The scope of salvation is enlarged to include not only spiritual concerns but material concerns as well. Hence the poor, the oppressed, and the voiceless are the ones in whom liberation theologians are interested. Third, the tools of liberation theology are not biblical studies and philosophy, but social sciences. Sociology, anthropology, economics, and political science form the cognitive foundation upon which this theology is built. Fourth, liberation theology emphasizes the reality of conflict in the world; the world is not seen as being peaceful. Conflict between the rich and the poor, the powerful and the oppressed, the upper class and the lower class is highlighted and an attempt is made to understand this conflict theologically. Fifth, liberation theology stresses praxis over theory. Theology is not something that one studies or writes about: theology is what one does. The mode of expression is *doing* theology. Sixth, liberation theology has been characterized by Brown and others as theology of the second act. By this is meant that theology consists of two acts—the first act is the commitment of one's life to God in Jesus Christ; the second act is one's reflection on what transpires because of the first act. In other words, personal faith necessarily results in corporate action. Liberation theology is, in the final analysis, an attempt to practice theology within the context of a socially unjust world. The personal concepts of sin and salvation are broadened to include corporate and social dimensions of reality.

Contextual Theology

C. S. Song, a Presbyterian from Taiwan, has emerged as one of the most creative spokespersons for contextual theology. Originally a student of Old Testament, Song later turned to theology and has done a remarkable job of blending the two fields together. Educated at National Taiwan University, New College at Edinburgh, and Union Theological Seminary in New York, Song has served as professor and principal of Tainan Theological College, as a visiting professor at Princeton Theological Seminary, and most recently with the World Council of Churches and the World Alliance of Reformed Churches in Geneva. During his time in the United States Song also worked as a denominational administrator in New York City and worked with Blacks in Mississippi. Although his theology is rooted in Asia, Song's international and cross-cultural experience gives his work a breadth not always found in contextual theologians.

Song's theology is best explained in his three books: *Christian Mission in Reconstruction: An Asian Attempt, Third-Eye Theology: Theology in Formation in Asian Settings*, and *The Compassionate God*.[12] These books form a theological trilogy in which Song reconstructs Christian mission from an Asian perspective, develops a theology from the vantage point of non-western Asian eyes, and finally points to the future in terms of a movement with the God of compassion. In all three books Song is concerned with what he calls a "theology of transposition," that is, a Christian theology transposed from its western context into the Asian context. According to Song there are several facets to this theological transposition—a shift in space and time, a means of communication, and most centrally, incarnation. This final step results in a theology that is thoroughly contextual, for there is no theological or ontological reason why Christian theology must be done in all times and places from the perspective of western philosophical categories and thought-forms.

In an early but significant essay entitled "From Israel to Asia—A Theological Leap," Song calls into question the traditional idea that all nations and cultures must somehow be included in one salvation history. He sees no reason why there may not be many salvation histories and why God may not work through other cultures even as he did in the culture and history of Israel.[13] Later, however, Song no longer uses the concept of salvation history; instead he uses biblical motifs of creation and redemption.[14] He understands creation and redemption as putting all cultures and religions on an equal footing in terms of God's grace and compassion. Song continues his theological development by speaking not only of creation and redemption but also of re-creation, where the Christian joins with God in the on-going task of creating a new heaven and a new earth.

The significance of contextual theology in general and of Song's theology in particular is that it takes seriously the historical and cultural context in which one lives and works. Not only are traditional theological answers understood in a different way, but the very questions asked vary from culture to culture. Thus contextual theology has both a hermeneutical and a constructive task. The Christian faith that has come to Asia, for example, through two thousand years of church history must be reinterpreted through Asian eyes, and theological questions posed which arise from the interaction of this reinterpretation of the Christian faith with a cultural and historical context. Song has addressed himself to both parts of this task—to the hermeneutical part in *Christian Mission in Reconstruction,* and to the constructive part in *Third-Eye Theology* and *The Compassionate God.* In dealing with the totality of the contextual theologian's task, Song presents a creative and outstanding example of how theology can and should be done in an Asian context.

Theological Pluralism Today

These four contemporary theological methodologies and the theological models representing them are, of course, by no means exhaustive, but they do point to one dramatic fact concerning the contemporary theological scene—it is highly pluralistic. Numerous options are available to any theological enquirer, from the traditional to the most radical. Furthermore, rather than being mutually exclusive, these methods often blend into various combinations. Jung Young Lee's book *The Theology of Change: A Christian Concept of God in an Eastern Perspective* is both contextual theology (dealing with Asian culture and history) and philosophical theology (using the Chinese philosophy of change as a foundation for theology).[15] Black theology in the United States speaks to a specific racial group in a given historical context but also focuses on liberation themes. It is not necessary, therefore, to use these methods and models in isolation from each other.

Each of these methods and models has strengths, particularly in an Asian context. One concern that many have about certain forms of contextual theology is the tendency to overlook theological doctrines such as the doctrine of the church. Contextual theologies may become so issue-oriented and localized that they lose sight of comprehensive Christian theology or forget that contextualization assumes there is something there to be contextualized. A firm grasp of systematic theology provides a balanced perspective that includes the totality of theology and serves as a safeguard against the ever-present dangers of syncretism and reductionism.

Process theology, with its fresh vision of the Christian faith, has done much to open the eyes of Asian students to the excitement of doing theology. Its openness to Buddhism and other forms of Asian thought make it especially suitable for cross-cultural and inter-religious dialogue.

Liberation theology raises the most controversy due to its involvement with politics, economics, and social structures. The fact that liberation theologians call for and even work for social change—sometimes to the point of taking up arms—has aroused great opposition. Obviously there is a real danger that theology become social gospel and the doctrines of sin and redemption become mere tools of those with political ambitions. At the same time, there can be no doubt that sin and redemption are both personal and corporate and that Christian commitment demands social action. Liberation theology keeps before the church the basic fact that theology is not only to be thought out—it is to be lived. It may well be, however, that contextual theology can add something of vital importance to liberation theology, for social change and the methods for achieving it must also be contextualized. What works in one culture may not work or even be desirable in another cultural context.

There is, of course, little that a westerner can write about applying contextual theology in Asia; this is a task for Asians. However, Asians and others from non-western cultures can teach westerners a great deal about theology. Westerners need to have their theological vision enlarged to include the whole church, not just the Latin church as it has come down through two thousand years of church history. Contextual theologians can have a part in this broadening process through sharing their theological insights with western colleagues. North Americans, especially, need to develop their own contextual theology. With the exception of Black theology and process theology, North American theology has been dominated by the theologies of Europe, especially Germany. Asians are developing their own theological consciousness; North Americans have yet to even arrive at that point. The theologians of Asia can, in a very real sense, become teachers in the ongoing process of theological contextualization in the West.

8

The Importance of
Christian Myth

In the West the world is dominated by our five senses; we believe only in what we can see, touch, hear, taste, or smell. We consider ourselves to be rationalists to the core, so that every possible idea and situation is subjected to a rigid scrutiny. We desire not opinions, legends, or dogmas but rather, facts. We want to know what really happened and consequently we sometimes make the mistake of believing that our rational materialistic approach apprehends the sum total of reality.

This error is dangerous for those engaged in the life and work of the church, academic or pastoral. One can easily end up by neglecting a vital element in the Christian gospel—that of myth. Our rationalistic worldview has tended to desacralize our worship until the average Protestant worship service focuses almost entirely upon a rational acceptance of the Christian gospel.

> The church leader feels himself under severe pressure to show the reasonableness of the Christian faith and teachings. He feels obliged to speak a language that is culturally accredited: the language of logical, discursive speech. Since myth is discredited as unscientific and illogical, he is urged

to avoid it, and the church corporately is encouraged to disown it. . . .
Rationality is the criterion for preaching. . . .[1]

The majority of mainstream Protestant churches, and certainly the majority of Reformed-Presbyterian Churches, have de-emphasized the sacraments, stripped the churches bare of almost all works of art, and almost totally neglected the mythical dimensions of the Christian gospel.

There are, of course, reasons for this emphasis upon the rational. The Reformers were reacting against abuses in the Church of Rome where ignorance abounded and an excessive emphasis was placed on the sacraments. Furthermore, the invention of the printing press meant that everyone could now have access to the Bible. This had a dramatic effect on the life of the church, for now laypeople could study the Bible on their own without relying on the official interpretation of the Church. The sermon took on a new importance in the worship service, and sharp debates began to arise among theologians and church leaders. With these changes came an emphasis upon rational understanding.

The Reinterpretation of Christian Myth

These new emphases gave rise to a shift in theological thinking. Scholars began to subject the Bible to a rationalistic examination, and numerous critical approaches began to appear, so that by the nineteenth century the critical-historical method had made deep inroads into the theological faculties of most European universities. Advancements in various sciences called into question many traditionally accepted biblical narratives, among them the stories of creation, the flood, the virgin birth, the literal resurrection, and the second coming of Christ. To many the conclusion from all this was obvious—those aspects of the Christian gospel which were in conflict with the modern worldview must either be radically reinterpreted or totally discarded.

The most significant twentieth-century theologian who held to this view was Rudolf Bultmann, who declared that "the cosmology of the New Testament is essentially mythical in character."[2] The New Testament world is one of angels, demons, supernatural miracles, and heavenly visions; "to this extent *the kerygma is incredible to modern man, for he is convinced that the mythical view of the world is obsolete.*"[3]

Bultmann concludes that "theology must undertake the task of stripping the Kerygma from its mythical framework, of 'demythologizing' it."[4] By this he does not mean to eliminate myth from the Christian gospel, but rather to reinterpret the meaning enshrined in myths within the framework of the modern world view.

This crucial point concerning Bultmann's thought cannot be over-emphasized, for it is precisely at this point that Bultmann is most frequently misunderstood. He is not discarding myth, but reinterpreting it to fit the modern worldview.

> Hence the importance of the New Testament mythology lies not in its imagery but in the understanding of existence which it enshrines. The real question is whether this understanding of existence is true. Faith claims that it is, and faith ought not to be tied down to the imagery of New Testament mythology.[5]

In this sense Bultmann has performed an important service to the church in that he has differentiated between the mythical world view and the understanding of existence enshrined in the myths.

Among many church circles, however, the mere mention of the word "myth" in connection with the Bible arouses immediate suspicion and mistrust. To many people myth is synonymous with fairy tale; to describe the creation in the Garden of Eden or the resurrection of Jesus as myth is to deny the historicity of these events. While it is true that some in the church do deny the historicity of these events, including some theologians, it by no means follows that just because an event is mythical then it is also non-historical. Hence there is no reason why the mythical elements of the Christian gospel should be excised from the life and work of the church.

It is, of course, questionable whether modern humanity is in fact convinced that the mythical view of the world is obsolete. The popularity of mythical themes in modern literature and drama and the increasing importance of the depth psychology of Carl Jung tend to contradict this view, as would the prevalence of the mythical theme of good and evil in conflict portrayed in modern films and television programs. Recent interest in witchcraft, demon possession, parapsychology, and astrology serves only to confirm that modern people are still very much fascinated by and involved in the mythical and that myth continues to play a significant role in human affairs.

One notices this dramatically in Asia, where myth is very much alive and forms a part of everyday existence for the majority of people. The countryside is literally dotted with shrines and temples, and every town has its share of fortune-tellers, exorcists, shamans, and faith healers. Many peoples of Asia have legends in which they are said to have descended from the gods. Temple carvings and paintings dramatically detail ancient myths. It is somewhat sobering for westerners to realize that their critical, rationalistic view of reality is, when all the cultures of the world are taken into account, a distinctly minority position.

Today we are beginning to discover in a most disconcerting manner that "myth is necessary because reality is so much larger than rationality."[6] In a world of many crises—the energy crisis, the population explosion, the constant threat of nuclear warfare, the destruction of the natural environment, the waste of the earth's natural resources—we see that we were wrong not to listen to the prophets, poets, sages, those whose outlook on life seems archaic and out of step with the fast pace of modern living. We have forgotten the mythic roots of our culture and, most of all, of our religion.

> Scientific rationalism tended to demythologize the cosmic drama, desacralize the universe, depersonalize truth, and decompose reality. Creation became physical and chemical process, not purpose; truth became whatever could be scientifically verified; and reality came to consist of bits and pieces that might or might not fit together. To speak in a mythical or poetic way was to the rationalist mind not to be taken seriously. At best it was extravagant speech and therefore incredible; at worst it was an admission of superstition.[7]

As Christian ministers, teachers, and especially theologians, we would do well to reconsider the importance of Christian myth, to reaffirm again that according to the Christian gospel creation does involve purpose, truth does not always rest with what can be scientifically verified, and reality does fit together under the lordship of an omnipotent God.

If we are going to recover the importance of Christian myth, we must first be clear about the definition of myth. The term "myth" does not necessarily mean untrue or unhistorical. Therefore, to use the terms "myth" and "mythical" in relation to biblical events such as the resurrection does not mean that these events did not take place within history.

Myth is to be defined as a complex of stories—some no doubt fact, and some fantasy—which, for various reasons, human beings regard as demonstrations of the inner meaning of the universe and human life. Myth is quite different from philosophy in the sense of abstract concepts, for the form of myth is always concrete—consisting of vivid, sensually intelligible narratives, images, rites, ceremonies, and symbols. A great deal of myth may therefore be based on historical events, but not all such events acquire the mythic character.[8]

From this standpoint we can see that the death and resurrection narratives concerning Jesus have mythical aspects. The passion narratives are vivid in their imagery and contain within them the basis for the doctrine of salvation which forms the very heart of the Christian gospel. In addition they serve as the foundation for the entire liturgical observances of Holy Week and the sacrament of the Eucharist. Finally, they form one of the major elements in the account of the Incarnation. There can be no doubt that the passion and resurrection narratives demonstrate the inner meaning of the universe and human life, for they tell of events which have "a miraculous or 'numinous' quality which marks them as special, queer, out of the ordinary, and therefore representative of the powers or Power behind the world."[9] For this reason people remember the passion and resurrection narratives while tending to forget various theological interpretations of those narratives. Indeed, interpretations come and go, but the stories themselves live on through the centuries.

The same can be said of the creation narratives, the story of the birth of Jesus, and the awesome eschatological themes found in the book of Revelation. These narratives have a mythical dimension, have become "a particular kind of story which has value in itself—a value independent of its embodiment in any literary work."[10] Taken from their biblical context, these narratives form the very basis of western culture as expressed in its art, literature, and music.

This is illustrated by the Narnia Chronicles of C. S. Lewis, a series of fairy tales which incorporate the mythical themes of the Christian faith. Significantly, these stories have hit a responsive chord with Chinese readers who would otherwise find Christian theology difficult and uninteresting.[11] While abstract theological doctrine is unattractive to the Chinese mind, the world of mythology is not: many Chinese readers could identify with the mythic elements in Christianity as rendered by C. S. Lewis and discover similar themes in their own mythologies. Christian myth is, therefore, an important element in the cross-cultural communication of the Christian faith.

The Characteristics of Myth

C. S. Lewis sets forth six characteristics of myth which, when applied to biblical narratives such as those of the passion and resurrection, decisively demonstrate their mythical nature.[12] First, a myth is extra-literary. It can stand apart from the work in which it is found and still convey its meaning. The fact that literally millions of people who have never read the Bible feel compelled to attend worship services on Easter Sunday shows the mythical significance of the resurrection narrative.

Second, "the pleasure of myth depends hardly at all on such usual narrative attractions as suspense or surprise."[13] In the passion narratives, for example, it is quite clear that the resurrection is in the offing; there is no suspense whatsoever. Yet in spite of this lack of suspense, the Gospels continue to be read and to impact culture far more than any novel or detective story filled with suspense.

Third, in a myth "human sympathy is at a minimum. We do not project ourselves at all strongly into the characters."[14] The passion narratives say little about the actual physical and emotional sufferings of Jesus. We do not feel sympathy for him nor question the justice of God's sending his only son to suffer such a horrible death. Nor does the story evoke sympathy for Judas, whose part was so essential.

Fourth, myth is "in one sense of that word, 'fantastic.' It deals with impossibilities and preternaturals."[15] Even prior to his birth, the life of Jesus is involved with preternatural experiences—the vision and dumbness of Zechariah, the birth of John, angels appearing to Mary and later to the shepherds, the virgin birth, and the star in the East. The story of the birth, life, death, and resurrection of Jesus is indeed fantastic.

Fifth, in myth "the experience may be sad or joyful but it is always grave. Comic myth . . . is impossible."[16] Myths deal with concepts, issues, and events which are of vital importance and therefore not to be taken lightly. The absence of comedy or humor in the four Gospels can be understood in this light, and it may partially account for the fact that artists rarely depict Jesus with even the hint of a smile, let alone a laugh.

Finally, the mythical experience inspires awe. "We feel it to be numinous. It is as if something of great moment had been communicated to us."[17] This is partially due to the fact that "the reality of the mythical, timeless event enters into the present moment of time."[18] What happened many years ago suddenly seems to be taking place before our very eyes.

> In so far, then, as the inner life of Christianity—the contemplation of God—is not just the reverent remembering of a past history, but the recurrent celebration and reliving of a timeless truth, it is possible for us to discuss the Christian story as something more profound than mere facts which once happened, to give it not only the status of history but also the tremendous dignity of myth, which is "once upon a time" in the sense that it is behind all time.[19]

For this reason we follow the liturgical cycles of the Christian year and observe the Eucharist. For this reason we celebrate Easter. We are not merely remembering events which took place almost two thousand years ago—we are taking part in something which transcends time and space. If we fail to include the mythical in our religious faith and practice we will be unable to experience this dimension of transcendence: we will be left with only lifeless historical facts. To neglect the mythical in our understanding of the resurrection is to deny its timelessness and power.[20]

J.R.R. Tolkien says that the Gospels "contain many marvels—particularly artistic, beautiful, and moving: 'mythical' in their perfect, self-contained significance; and at the same time powerfully symbolic and allegorical. . . ."[21] In a day when this mythical element is so often missing in the life and work of the church, our approach to these great biblical narratives must be more than rational, for the totality of reality includes much, much more. The church must be able to bring the gospel message to bear on all of reality. As it is, we are speaking to only a part of human reality—the rational. The consequences of this have been grave. "Protestantism today is adrift because it has misjudged the cultural climate and disowned the church's traditional language of myth. It has glimpsed the surface of rationalism but not paused to see the myths beneath."[22] This same theme is echoed in the words of Carl Jung:

> Can we not understand that all the outward tinkerings and improvements do not touch man's inner nature, and that everything ultimately depends upon whether the man who wields the science and the technics is *compos mentis* [sane in mind] or not? Christianity has shown us the way, but, as the facts bear witness, it has not penetrated deeply enough below the surface.[23]

The message to the church is quite clear. Myth is a part of human existence; a part that lies buried in the unconscious and therefore cannot be swept away by a rationalistic world view. Christianity contains numerous mythical elements which are necessary for a balanced and complete understanding of the gospel message. To present the rational without the mythical or vice versa is to do a great injustice to the totality of the Christian faith. This is a tragedy in the West, where we have suppressed the mythical in favor of the rational; in the East it is a crime, for rich mythical traditions already present in the culture are ignored and denied. Christian myth is important if we are to recover the timelessness and the power of the life and witness of Jesus, for "once the value of the mythic perspective is acknowledged, the church's mission can recover a dimension that is inherent in both the gospel and the modern world."[24]

9

The Rational and
the Mystical in
Theological Construction

The relationship between the rational and the mystical has been a constant source of tension in eastern as well as western theological construction. The categories of the rational and the mystical are common to both East and West, but the ways each have defined the relationship between reason and myth in religion has been consistent with cultural thought.

Synthesis: The Chinese Way

Chinese philosophical and religious thought is characterized by its avoidance of extremes. "One of the outstanding facts in the history of Chinese philosophy has been its tendency and ability to synthesize."[1] There may be extremes to be sure, but always in the end the pendulum swings back toward the middle. On the Chinese mainland, for example, we have seen the extremes of Maoism and the cultural revolution give way to an opening up to the outside world and the official resurrection of Confucius as one of China's greatest teachers. Religion, which was once condemned, is now tolerated, and westernization—even capitalism—which was previously spurned is now encouraged, within certain prescribed limits. The Mean is once again asserting itself as a dominant principle of Chinese life and thought.

Perhaps the clearest example of this avoidance of extremes and tendency toward synthesis is to be found in the Chinese acceptance of both Confucianism, with its emphasis upon the rational, and Taoism, with its stress upon the mystical. At first glance they are quite different. Confucianism is humanistic in its orientation and deals with ethics and the social life. The Confucianist is concerned with a rational working out of various ethical laws which enable society to function in an orderly manner. The Confucian ideal is to fulfill one's family obligations, to serve the state to the best of one's ability, and to live harmoniously in society. For the Confucianist the Tao or Way refers to the proper way of life for social humanity.[2] Taoism, on the other hand, is oriented toward a mystical and intuitive understanding of the realm of nature. The Taoist seeks to know the order of the natural world in order to live in harmony with nature. While Confucian education stresses a rational memorization of the classics, Taoism emphasizes a kind of mystical union with nature and knowledge by means of intuition. The Taoist ideal is not to live in society but to escape from society into the mountains and live as a sage, contemplating the essence of nature. Thus "for the Taoists the Tao or Way was not the right way of life within human society, but the way the universe worked; in other words, the *Order of Nature*."[3] These two seemingly contradictory ways of life were often synthesized in the Confucian scholar who lived a fruitful life as head of his family and in service of the state, then retired in his later years to the mountains to take up brush painting and calligraphy as a Taoist sage.

One of the reasons these two schools of thought co-exist is that both maintain a common theory of the relationship between extremes: "This is that both in the sphere of nature and in that of man, when the development of anything brings it to one extreme, a reversal to the other extreme takes place; that is, to borrow an expression from Hegel, everything involves its own negation."[4] Furthermore, both schools of thought are influenced by the concept of Yin and Yang which has left its mark on virtually every facet of Chinese life and thought.

No aspect of Chinese civilization—whether metaphysics, medicine, government, or art—has escaped its imprint. In simple terms, the doctrine teaches that all things and all events are products of two elements, forces, or principles: yin, which is negative, passive, weak and destructive, and yang, which is positive, active, strong and constructive.[5]

> Philosophically, however, it resulted not only in the concept of a common law governing both man and Nature but also in a most important doctrine that has dominated Chinese philosophy in the last eight hundred years, namely, the unity of man and Nature, or "Nature and man forming one body."[6]

The result is two dipolar opposites, each of which involves its own negation, yet each of which by necessity forms a unity with the other.

The Problem of Western Dualism

Western thought deals with the question of opposites from a decidedly different perspective. Whereas the Asian speaks of "both/and," the westerner uses "either/or." Thus in theology one frequently comes across such phrases as Jerusalem or Athens, God or mammon, Law or Gospel, children of light or children of darkness, and heaven or hell. In each of these dichotomies it is tacitly understood that each category is mutually exclusive, although each category would be meaningless without the possibility of its negation.

Western thought has resulted in a variety of dualisms. Herman Dooyeweerd and his followers have isolated three in the history of western philosophical thought: the form-matter dualism of the ancient Greeks, the nature-grace dualism of the Scholastics, and the nature-freedom dualism of the modern humanists.[7] Various means have been proposed to overcome these dualisms. Dooyeweerd proposes a Christian philosophy based upon biblical categories of creation, fall, and redemption.[8] In his attempt to overcome the form-matter dualism, however, he is faced with the theological problem of the body-soul dualism and the supposed immortality of the soul.[9]

Another western attempt to overcome dualism is the method of dialectics first proposed by G. W. F. Hegel. According to Hegel one begins with a thesis, moves to an antithesis, and then brings the two together in a synthesis. Dialectics does not apply, however, in the case of contradictions.

> The sort of system which grounds the method is not the sort within which the principle of contradiction obtains. Contradictories cannot be dialectically resolved; between them there is no ground of synthesis. But such systems are abstract, that is, exemplified only in formal deductions; they are lacking in factual content. Dialectical analysis is possible only within systems which are factual, that is, constituted by statements of fact and statements of possibility grounded in fact. Here the principle of contrariety, not the principle of contradiction obtains; and dialectical analysis is identical with the resolution of contraries. Here and here alone, is the dialectical method applicable; and it alone is applicable here.[10]

One must conclude, therefore, that either the supposed contradictories are in fact contraries, or that the contradictories cannot be brought into synthesis by means of dialectic. In either case the problem of dualism remains.

Thus dualism between the rational and the mystical has been a particular problem for western theology. Rationalists have tended to be suspicious of mystics, accusing them of blurring the distinction between Creator and creature and the subject and object (two more dualisms).[11] Mystics, on the other hand, contend that the rationalists are narrow-minded and close their eyes to the primal religious experience common to all the world's great religions.[12] This dualism intensified with the Protestant Reformation's emphasis upon the Scriptures. The Catholic tradition, while somewhat suspicious of mysticism, did make a place for it in the church. Within the institution of monasticism, mystics were able to function under the authority of the church. Also the Catholic mass, particularly in the doctrine of transubstantiation, contained mystical elements. In reaction to Catholic excesses, Protestants abolished monasticism and rejected the doctrine of transubstantiation, thus in effect denying mysticism any avenues of expression. The emphasis was now upon Scripture and a rational understanding of it. In the Catholic Church mysticism was allowed, but within confines of established rational theological tradition; among Protestants the emphasis upon the rational left no room for the mystical at all.

Overcoming Dualism

Confucian scholars traditionally have played down the role of the mystical in Chinese thought and have instead emphasized the significance of the rational. Many such scholars have asserted that the Chinese are, in general, a non-religious people, a view that continues to characterize the attitude of many modern Chinese intellectuals. This view was especially strong in the 1920s when the intellectual community looked to the West with its technology and scientific method. The mystical was seen as both superstitious and humiliating.[13] If China was to progress as a nation it must rid itself of all mystical elements and adopt the rationalistic scientific method of the West. Only in this way could China take its place in the modern world. In Taiwan today there are many who consider the religious traditions of Taiwan to be mere superstitions which stand in the way of full modernization and sound economic development. On the mainland the official view, Marxist materialism, tolerates religion as something for those few who really do not know better.

Yet in his study of religion on mainland China, C. K. Yang found that "there was not one corner in the vast land of China where one did not find temples, shrines, altars, and other places of worship. The temples and shrines dotting the entire landscape were a visible indication of the strong and pervasive influence of religion in Chinese society, for they stood as symbols of a social reality."[14] According to Yang, rationalism was at the heart of the characterization of China as nonreligious.

> Much of the underestimation of religion in China stems from the rationalistic features of Confucianism. But the rationalistic qualities of Confucianism alone did not appear adequate to meet the challenge from the vast domain of the unknown, to explain convincingly the extraordinary phenomena of society and nature, to deal with frustration and shock from tragedies in the crises of life, including death, to lift man's spirit above the level of selfish and utilitarian involvement in the mundane world so as to give to man a higher cause for unity and harmony with his fellow man, or to justify the enduring soundness of the moral order in the face of morally unaccountable success and failure. These and other associated questions of life and society led to the inevitable development of religion in China, as in other cultures.[15]

Even the casual observer in Taiwan cannot help but notice the many shrines and temples, including those under construction, which testify to the strength of religion in a supposedly secular society. It is clear, then, that the mystical has not disappeared from the Chinese scene, westernization and economic development notwithstanding.

For Christians in Taiwan this persistent presence of the mystical poses a special problem, for not only has Confucianism opposed the mystical, but much of western Christianity has done so as well. Since the Enlightenment and the rise of the scientific method, western theology has become increasingly rational.[16] This has been particularly true of the Reformed tradition, which has a well-developed history of rationalism going back to the Reformed Scholasticism of the seventeenth century.[17] Rationalistic Reformed theology has come to Taiwan and other areas of Asia by way of Scotland (common sense realism), Princeton Theological Seminary (the Old Princeton theology of Alexander, Hodge, and Warfield), Union Theological Seminary in Virginia (the conservative theology of Dabney), Westminster Theological Seminary (the Westminster theology of Van Til), and missionaries. This theology reflects the culture from which it has come, a culture which is rational and scientific in its worldview.[18]

Aside from the Confucian intelligentsia, the majority of the Taiwan population holds to a worldview that is decidedly mystical and non-rational.[19] Common to this worldview is a belief in spirits, various kinds of gods and goddesses, miracles, and the possibility of direct communication with the supernatural through the use of shamans or spirit mediums. This essentially mystical worldview forms the cultural matrix of the average Taiwanese, both Christian and non-Christian. In the church the rationalistic worldview of western theology has been superimposed upon this mystical worldview so that the two worldviews coexist side by side.

This coexistence has had several interesting results. There are those Christians who have become completely westernized and have fully adopted the rationalistic theology of the West. Others have attempted to work out a synthesis of the two positions, but in doing so have sometimes opened themselves to charges of syncretism. One of the most creative and successful of these syntheses is the so-called Spirit Movement found in many of the mountain churches. Here the social functions of the traditional shamans have been maintained but at the same time the monotheism of Christian theology has been affirmed so that the "spirits" have been replaced by the Holy Spirit. This unique blending of the rational and the mystical has not been without price, however, for the mountain churches once split over the issue into two groups—those who followed the Spirit Movement and those who did not. But in time the wound was healed and the two factions are now reunited in full communion and fellowship with each other.

By far the more common result is the division of reality into two distinct spheres of influence—the rational and the mystical. "Village Christianity today emphasizes an understanding of life in moral categories and in a rational manner. The mysterious influences of spirits, demons, or gods are excluded from the world. The sphere of God is the world beyond."[20] In a very real sense, then, western theology has imposed a dualism upon a people whose previous worldview was characterized by the principle of dipolarity, a principle that "was one of the most fruitful and useful ever devised by the mind of man for making sense out of the infinite multitude of diverse facts in the universe."[21]

Ironically, the way out of this dualistic dilemma is to be found in the very scientific method that produced it in the first place, for it is the scientists who are now calling into question the western dualism between the rational and the mystical. Indeed, it is scientists who are now saying that the concepts of Yin and Yang and the principle of dipolarity form a more accurate description of reality than the dualism of old. These new insights come primarily from two sources—brain research and high energy particle physics.

It is, of course, common knowledge that the brain has two hemispheres: "The left hemisphere processes information sequentially; the right hemisphere simultaneously, accessing several inputs at once. The left hemisphere works in series; the right in parallel. The left hemisphere is something like a digital computer; the right like an analog computer."[22] The left hemisphere is more rational and deals with cause and effect; the right hemisphere is more intuitive and controls holistic change. Almost immediately one can see that the West has tended to emphasize the left hemisphere and the East the right hemisphere. Robert Ornstein of the Langley Porter Neuropsychiatric Institute in San Francisco points out why the West has emphasized the left hemisphere and largely ignored the right.

> Ornstein . . . suggests that our awareness of right hemisphere function is a little like our ability to see stars in the daytime. The sun is so bright that the stars are invisible, despite the fact that they are just as present in our

sky in the daytime as at night. When the sun sets, we are able to perceive the stars. In the same way, the brilliance of our most recent evolutionary accretion, the verbal abilities of the left hemisphere, obscures our awareness of the functions of the intuitive right hemisphere, which in our ancestors must have been the principal means of perceiving the world.[23]

Hence it is language and the writing technologies associated with it that cause a disproportionate emphasis upon the left hemisphere.

It is no accident that the Reformation coincided with the development of the printing press in Europe so that everyone could have a Bible of their own. The individual could now receive revelation through the medium of the written word and no longer had to depend exclusively upon the priesthood and the mass. The ordained clergy and the sacraments were still in effect, but now they were overshadowed by the written word which was freely available to all. In like manner, Confucius stressed the availability of education to all and his followers made the classics the basis of the Confucian educational system. Hence the state civil religion "owed to the Confucian classics its possession of a basis of dogma governing its development."[24] In both Reformed theology and Confucianism the written word became the foundation of rationalism.

Recent brain research suggests that the mutual distrust between rationalists and mystics has a biological basis rather than simply a cultural or doctrinal one. The left hemisphere seems to feel quite defensive—in a strange way insecure—about the right hemisphere; and, if this is so, verbal criticism of intuitive thinking becomes suspect on the ground of motive. Unfortunately, there is every reason to think that the right hemisphere has comparable misgivings—expressed nonverbally, of course—about the left.[25] Seen in this light, the Chinese principle of dipolarity was a highly significant advance in human thought, for it brought together that which is naturally in a state of tension.

Contemporary research in high energy particle physics has also called into question the dualism of western thought. As new discoveries are made in physics and old theories are replaced by new ones, it becomes increasingly clear that "physicists have 'proved,' rationally, that our rational ideas about the world in which we live are profoundly deficient."[26] Central to these new insights is what is called quantum mechanics. Without entering into a technical discussion of physics, we can say that quantum mechanics asserts that "pure experience is never restricted to merely two possibilities. Our *conceptualization* of a given situation may create the illusion that each dilemma has only two horns, but this illusion is caused by assuming that experience is bound by the same rules as symbols."[27] While we may think in terms of either/or categories, experience itself is never limited in this way; there is always an alternative between every "either" and every "or."

Related to quantum mechanics is Bell's theorem, first proposed by J. S. Bell in 1964.

> Bell's theorem is a mathematical construct which, as such, is indecipherable to the nonmathematician. Its implications, however, could affect profoundly our basic world view. Some physicists are convinced that it is the most important single work, perhaps, in the history of physics. One of the implications of Bell's theorem is that, at a deep and fundamental level, the "separate parts" of the universe are connected in an intimate and immediate way.
>
> In short, Bell's theorem and the enlightened experience of unity are very compatible.[28]

What the new physicists are saying is that the mystical vision of the world is in fact closer to reality than the rationalistic scientific view so that "one is led to a new notion of *unbroken wholeness* which denies the classical idea of analyzability of the world into separately and independently existent parts."[29] Modern physics is asserting that the rational view of the world is, in actual fact, not the way the world is at all; on the level of sub-atomic particles the world is irrational and mystical.

All of this has profound implications for theological construction. We have pointed out that the current dialogue partners with theology are Scripture and the creeds of the churches (systematic theology), philosophy (philosophical theology), culture (contextual theology), and the social sciences (political theology). Given the insights arising from brain research, high energy particle physics, and other scientific endeavors, it would seem that a new method of theological construction with science as the dialogue partner is not only possible but imperative. Theology cannot ignore the fact that much of what we thought concerning the nature of reality is in the realm of symbol rather than in the realm of actual experience.

Such a method of theological construction would do justice to both the rationalism of the West and the mysticism of the East. It would provide a way of understanding the relationship between the either/or of the West and the both/and of the East, while at the same time making us aware that there is a biological basis for both points of view. Since science is transcultural—the canons of science operate in the same manner no matter what the cultural context—theological construction using science as a dialogue partner could provide the first step toward a truly universal and transcultural theology.[30]

Paradoxically, current scientific research is vindicating some of the oldest religious concepts and practices known. Rather than being destructive of theology, science is affirming theology. After attending a conference at the Lawrence Berkeley Laboratory in Berkeley, California, Gary Zukav wrote: "To my great surprise, I discovered that (1), I understood everything that they [the physicists] said, and (2), their discussion sounded very much like a theological discussion."[31] Religion and science need not be contradictory for, if the world is one, the dimensions of reality will not contradict each other.

As recent scientific discoveries open up new and creative possibilities in terms of theological interpretation, traditional doctrines are taking on new meaning. A reaffirmation of the concept of dipolarity can provide a way of overcoming many of the dualisms that have plagued theology for centuries. Most important, the rational and the mystical can be brought together for the purpose of theological life and work.

Word and Sacrament

From the perspective of Reformed theology in Asia in general and in Taiwan in particular, no doctrine is more in need of creative reinterpretation than that of Word and Sacrament. The Presbyterian Church in Taiwan is Reformed in its theology both by virtue of its heritage and its commitment, and as such it affirms the belief that the two means of grace are Word and Sacrament. Both are considered to be equally important to the life and work of the church, yet in actual practice the Word is given considerable precedence over the Sacraments. In most churches the Bible is prominently displayed in the front of the church, either on the communion table or on an altar especially made for that purpose. The baptismal font is frequently hidden away in a corner (often topped with a vase of flowers) or absent altogether, and only rarely is a communion chalice visible. The Bible is faithfully read at each service and the sermon is generally an exposition of a passage of Scripture. The sacrament of communion, however, is administered quarterly or, in a few churches, monthly. In almost no instances it is administered on a weekly basis. In most Presbyterian churches the sermon, which is by its very nature rational, serves as the focal point of the worship service. Even the weekly prayer meetings are largely devoted to Bible study. There is almost no place in the life and worship of the average Presbyterian church to express the mystical.

The fact that both Word and Sacrament are understood as means of grace is ample evidence that Reformed theology is dipolar in its foundational structure. What has happened is that the emphasis upon language and the written Word has caused the mystical and intuitional side to atrophy. It was not always this way, however, for John Calvin was firmly convinced of the mystical aspect of God's communication to humankind through the power of the Holy Spirit. In a "Summary of Doctrine Concerning the Ministry of the Word and Sacraments" Calvin states that "we believe this communication to be (a) mystical, and incomprehensible to human reason, and (b) spiritual, since it is effected by the Holy Spirit; . . ."[32] Furthermore, "to effect this union, the Holy Spirit uses a double instrument, the preaching of the Word and the administration of the sacraments."[33] Calvin goes on to distinguish between the external minister (the rational) and the internal minister (the mystical). The external minister is the pastor who preaches the Word, baptizes with water, and gives the bread and wine. The internal minister is the Holy Spirit who truly communicates, baptizes with Christ's blood, and feeds the souls of the faithful.[34] The dipolar relationship between Word and Sacrament is affirmed by Calvin when he says "that the right administering of the Sacrament cannot stand apart from the Word. For whatever benefit may come to us from the Supper requires the Word: whether we are to be confirmed in faith, or exercised in confession, or aroused to duty, there is a need for preaching."[35] The mystical is not mere superstition or magic; it is practiced and understood in relationship to the rational Word.

Unlike most Presbyterians today, Calvin was strongly in favor of weekly communion.

It would be well to require that the Communion of the Holy Supper of Jesus Christ be held every Sunday at least as a rule. When the Church assembles together for the great consolation which the faithful receive and the profit which proceeds from it, in every respect according to the promises which are there presented to our faith, then we are really made participants of the body and blood of Jesus, of his death, of his life, of his Spirit and of all his benefits.[36]

The table of the Lord ought to be spread in the sacred assembly at least once a week.[37]

Therefore, the custom ought to be well established in all Churches, of celebrating the Supper as frequently as the capacity of the people will allow.[38]

In Calvin's view the Sacrament of the Lord's Supper "was ordained to be frequently used among all Christians" and he cites Acts 2:42 where the early church met for the preaching of the Word, prayer, partaking of the Supper, and almsgiving.[39] Obviously, the Sacrament of Baptism can be observed only when there are candidates suitably prepared to receive the sacrament. But here too, it should be administered whenever needed and in conjunction with study of and knowledge of the Word. For Calvin, Word and Sacrament were of equal importance and were to be an integral part of the weekly service of worship in the churches.

As Reformed churches became more scholastic in their theology, the Word soon overshadowed the Sacrament. "The Reformation went a long way in the direction we have moved: by reducing to two the number of the sacraments, by its emphasis on the sermon as the central means, as well as by its freedom in its treatment of the offices. Its biblicism, however, soon restricted this development."[40] This biblicism continues to have an influence upon the Reformed view of Scripture. Hence Karl Barth poses the following question: "Since the means of grace is fundamentally one, why does it take a twofold form? Is it because of the weakness of faith that in addition to the Word the sacrament is also needed as a personal application of the Word?"[41] G. C. Berkouwer replies as follows: "And because the Word of the gospel is important, so also is the sacrament. It does not come as a secondary—in the sense of unimportant—addition, but it becomes important because it is fully directed toward the richness of the Word and toward the trustworthiness of that Word. The secondary sacrament is, because of its absolute directness toward the primary Word, absolutely important."[42] Even in such contemporary theologians as Barth and Berkouwer, we still find the subordination of Sacrament to Word, of the mystical to the rational.

A possible way out of this unequal relationship is to be found in Hendrikus Berkhof's idea of the duality of revelation.

> To God's coming down into our world must therefore correspond a creative leap of our cognition beyond its own limitations. Both a heightening and a liberation of our cognitive faculty are needed; and that is beyond our ability. Beside the revelation we need the illumination of our mind to be able to perceive the supernatural in the natural and the divine majesty in the humiliation. No revelation will be effected unless God works in us this double revelational activity. He must make himself present in our reality *and* he must open our eyes to make us see his presence.
>
> For this double activity dogmatics uses the concepts *Word* and *Spirit*. Separately as well as together, both play a large role in the Bible. There Word is often used as the denominator for the whole of the revelational event. Yet revelation is by no means always in the form of words; it happens also in events, visions, cultic rites, and (in Christ) in a person. By labeling all this as "word," the communicative nature of revelation receives all the emphasis; it happens as an appeal to our existence, and it wants to be heard, understood, and obeyed. But if the latter does indeed take place, the word event, the speaking of that word, has apparently been augmented by another event, the hearing of the word. To bring that about is the work of the Spirit, that is, of God who not only comes to us from the outside, but who is also the one who transforms our life and our existence, giving us ears and enabling us to let him come to us as the speaking and revealing God.[43]

From this perspective Word and Spirit are two forms of revelation and one is not subordinate to the other. The Word, which is rational, coexists on an equal basis with the Spirit, which is mystical and beyond our own cognitive limitations. Furthermore, this Spirit also includes Sacrament, since revelation goes beyond Word to include events, visions, and cultic rites. Berkhof's concept of revelation is both scientifically correct in that it is dipolar in nature, and closer to the views of Calvin in that it involves both the rational and the mystical—the Word and the Spirit.

The recovery of a dipolar understanding of Word and Sacrament will restore to the church in both the East and the West the fullness of its Reformed theological heritage as well as provide the church with a means of ministering to the entire congregation, not just to that portion of the congregation which responds well to a rational approach. In a very real sense, congregations would then be given the opportunity to make use of both hemispheres of the brain in worship. Furthermore, a full recovery of the position and role of Sacrament in Reformed life and worship would open up numerous possibilities for creative theological construction within the Asian context.[44] By demonstrating, in the weekly worship service, that Word and Sacrament are both essential and important, Presbyterians in Taiwan—and Christians in all of Asia—could take a significant step toward the reconciliation of the rational and the mystical, thus affirming the wholeness of the human person, created in the image and likeness of God.

10

A Look
to the Future

This completes my inquiry into thinking and doing theology from the perspective of a western theologian living and working in Asia. Against the background of five years in Taiwan, five years in Korea, and five months in Hong Kong—during which time considerable effort was expended on questions of theological method—I have singled out several areas of significance for theological construction. These include spirituality, language, hermeneutics, myth, culture, and philosophy, models for doing theology, and the relation between the rational and the mystical. I have also considered the theologian as a person and as a change agent in a cross-cultural situation. The question I must address now is: what does all this really mean for doing theology?

One way of answering this question is to cite an example of actual theological work. In the mid-1970s a theological consultation was held in the Philippines on the subject of spirituality in Asia. A number of papers were either circulated or read at the conference. In the days following the consultation, when the organizers were engaged in the process of evaluation, it became obvious that two of the papers from the consultation were especially provocative and stimulating. In fact, these two papers were in a class by themselves. The author of one was a western missionary teaching on the faculty of an Asian theological seminary. The author of the other was an Asian who had spent several years in the West while engaged in graduate study. Both authors had significant cross-cultural experience which enabled them to take a critical stance toward their own cultures while at the same time being open to and appreciative of cultures different from their own. The cross-cultural viewpoint gave their papers a depth lacking in the other presentations.

I suggest, therefore, that theological work in the future will move more and more in a cross-cultural direction. For too long the church has been held captive by culture-bound theologies. The self-imposed "universalism" of western theologies is only one example, for today there are numerous localized contextual theologies that are as culture-bound as the theologies of the West.

> A contextual theology related to one group, nation, or region may be too narrow to respond to all the aspects of even a local problem. . . . Hence even the best of contextual theologies, related to a limited group or region, must be counterbalanced by more universal perspectives relating to the world as a whole.[1]

Western theologies have tended to be strong in the area of metaphysics, yet here the theologies of Asia have significant contributions to offer. Third World theologies have emphasized social change, yet it must be remembered that churches played an important role in the American Revolution and that Black theology has developed out of a North American context. If science were to become a significant dialogue partner with theology, this would go a long way toward universalizing aspects of theology relating to the scientific enterprise. The experiential approach, as practiced by Thomas Merton and others, seeks to share in others' religious experience. This has enabled universal categories of religious experience to be identified from among the many particular expressions of religious life. As the world increasingly becomes a global village it is imperative that theologians keep the universal and the particular together in a creative tension, for out of this tension will come meaningful and relevant theology.

There are, of course, those in both East and West who have been and who are now thinking along these lines. Paul Tillich, in his last

public lecture asserted that "revelatory experiences are universally human" and that "there are revealing and saving powers in all religions.
God has not left himself unwitnessed."[2] Recent books by such scholars
as John Hick, Ninian Smart, and Wilfred Cantwell Smith have exam-
ined the idea from the perspective of the science of religion.[3] One of
the most promising contributions comes from the Sri Lankan theologian
Tissa Balasuriya, in his book *Planetary Theology.*[4] Balasuriya asserts
that virtually all social issues are global in scope, thus necessitating a
theological approach that is universal in perspective. Theological con-
sultations such as those held by the Christian Conference of Asia and
the World Council of Churches are bringing theologians and church
leaders together to consider common issues and concerns. Surely out
of this interchange of ideas, universal categories and themes will be
discovered and a truly global theology will begin to emerge.

A global theology will emerge, however, not from one context
attempting to impose its theology on the others, as was done in the past
by western theology. Rather, as various contexts come together and
share in an attitude of mutual respect, each will inform and teach the
others. There will, therefore, continue to be a great plurality of contextual theologies for "no definition of Christianity is absolute, for culture
itself is relative. There exists a mutual necessity between culture and
Christianity."[5]

A primary resource for contextual theologies has been and continues to be the kerygma, the central core of the Christian faith and gospel.

> This requires a direct return to the source of revelation—the Scriptures—
> especially to the person of Jesus Christ as we see him in the gospels. We
> must purify our minds of the restrictive Christendom-centered theologies
> that have blurred the universality of Jesus Christ. We must ask ourselves
> how we are to understand the gospels in our times.[6]

Hermeneutics, then, will play a vital role in the theological enterprise.

This in turn will emphasize the fact that theological construction
is an open-ended process, because "the resulting contextual theology is
always tentative for . . . knowledge of the Biblical message is limited
and . . . experience of the changing cultural situation always relative."[7]
Out of this interaction of Scripture and culture will emerge universal
metaphysical categories and universal issues of socio-economic and political concern. A global theology will develop as contextual theologies
interact and common themes and concerns are identified.

Both Asian and western theology have contributions to make toward this newly emerging theological consciousness. The task of Christian expatriates is, therefore, an important one, for they are on the front lines in the convergence of cultures, religious traditions, social issues, theologies, and—most importantly—people. In the final analysis, in theology it is people who are the most precious, and it is people for whom Christ lived, died, and lives today.

The task of thinking and doing theology, whether in Asia or elsewhere, is an exciting one in which all Christians are called to participate. It is none other than joining with God in the building of a new world and the realization of the kingdom.

Notes

1. The Theologian as a Caring Person

1. Kosuke Koyama, *Waterbuffalo Theology* (London: SCM Press, 1974), p. 130.
2. Gordon D. Kaufman, "Theological Method and Indigenization: Six Theses," *Shepherd's Staff*, No. 44 (June 1977), 6–18.
3. Peter L. Berger, *The Social Reality of Religion* (London: Faber & Faber, 1969), p. 3.
4. Helmut Thielicke, *A Little Exercise for Young Theologians*, tr. Charles L. Taylor (Grand Rapids: Eerdmans, 1962), p. 37.
5. Paul Tillich, *Systematic Theology*, I (Chicago: University of Chicago Press, 1951), p. 4.
6. Berger, *The Social Reality of Religion*, p. 28.
7. Kaufman, "Theological Method and Indigenization: Six Thesis," p. 7.
8. Karl Barth, *Church Dogmatics*, I/1, tr. G. T. Thompson (Edinburgh: T. & T. Clark, 1936), p. 1.
9. Thielicke, *A Little Exercise for Young Theologians*, p. 34.
10. *Ibid.*, p. 25.
11. Tillich, *Systematic Theology*, I, p. 3.
12. Barth, *Church Dogmatics*, I/1, p. 1.
13. Tillich, *Systematic Theology*, I, p. 35.

14. Thielicke, *A Little Exercise for Young Theologians*, p. 35.
15. *Ibid.*, p. 31.
16. Tillich, *Systematic Theology*, I, p. 3.
17. Koyama, *Waterbuffalo Theology*, p. 131.

2. Doing Theology in the Concrete

1. A. C. Moule, *Christians in China Before the Year 1550* (New York: Octagon Books, 1977), pp. 24, 32.
2. *Ibid.*, p. 1.
3. The Chinese rites controversy is discussed in detail in Kenneth Scott Latourette, *A History of Christian Missions in China* (New York: Macmillan, 1929), pp. 131–155.
4. Two books dealing with the nineteenth-century and early twentieth-century Christian mission to China are: Paul A. Cohen, *China and Christianity: The Missionary Movement and the Growth of Chinese Antiforeignism, 1860–1870* (Cambridge: Harvard University Press, 1963) and John K. Fairbank, ed., *The Missionary Enterprise in China and America* (Cambridge: Harvard University Press, 1974).
5. Kosuke Koyama, *Waterbuffalo Theology* (London: SCM Press, 1974), pp. 209–224.
6. Nicola Trigault in Matthew Ricci, *China in the Sixteenth Century: The Journals of Matthew Ricci: 1583–1610*, compiled by Nicola Trigault, tr. Louis J. Gallagher, SJ (New York: Random House, 1953), pp. xi-xii.
7. George H. Dunne, SJ, *Generation of Giants: The Story of the Jesuits in China in the Last Decades of the Ming Dynasty* (Notre Dame, Indiana: University of Notre Dame Press, 1962), p. 88.
8. *Ibid.*, p. 28.
9. Arnold H. Rowbotham, *Missionary and Mandarin: The Jesuits at the Court of China* (Berkeley and Los Angeles: University of California Press, 1942), p. 63.
10. Vincent Cronin, *The Wise Man From the West* (New York: E. P. Dutton, 1955), p. 279.
11. Rowbotham, *Missionary and Mandarin*, p. 52.
12. Dunne, *Generation of Giants*, pp. 32–34
13. *Ibid.*, pp. 55–56.
14. Thomas Merton, *Mystics and Zen Masters* (New York: Dell Pub. Co., 1967), p. 83.
15. *Ibid.*, pp. 84–85.
16. Rowbotham, *Missionary and Mandarin*, p. 291.
17. Lawrence J. Burkholder, "Rethinking Christian Life and Mission in Light of the Chinese Experience" in *China and Christianity: Historical and Future Encounters,* ed. James D. Whitehead, Yu-Ming Shaw, N. J. Girardot (Notre Dame, Indiana: Center for Pastoral and Social Ministry, University of Notre Dame, 1979), p. 210.

18. Raymond L. Whitehead, "Christ, Salvation and Maoism" in *China and Christianity: Historical and Future Encounters,* ed. James D. Whitehead, Yu-Ming Shaw, N. J. Girardot (Notre Dame, Indiana: Center for Pastoral and Social Ministry, University of Notre Dame, 1979), p. 244.

3. The Search for a New Spirituality

1. See Emerito P. Nacpil, "Report of the Executive Director of ATSSEA," *South East Asia Journal of Theology,* Vol. 17, No. 1 (1976), 91–94 and "Minutes of the Executive Committee of ATSSEA" in the same issue, 53–54.

2. Thomas Merton, *Seeds of Destruction* (New York: Farrar, Straus and Giroux, 1964), pp. 287–288.

3. For an illuminating discussion of the demonic and negative element in religious experience see R. C. Zaehner, *Our Savage God* (London: Collins, 1974).

4. Herman Dooyeweerd, *In the Twilight of Western Thought* (Philadelphia: The Presbyterian and Reformed Publishing Co., 1960), pp. 1–34. Paul Tillich discusses this same idea in his *Theology of Culture,* ed. Robert C. Kimball (New York: Oxford University Press, 1959).

5. Thomas Merton speaks specifically to the problem of secularism and spirituality in *The Asian Journal of Thomas Merton,* ed. Naomi Burton, Patrick Hart, James Laughlin (New York: New Directions, 1973), pp. 326–343.

6. See Donald G. Bloesch, *The Ground of Certainty: Toward an Evangelical Theology of Revelation* (Grand Rapids: Eerdmans, 1971), pp. 140–155.

7. A detailed account of Buddhism and its relationship to Chinese culture is found in Kenneth K. S. Ch'en, *Buddhism in China: A Historical Survey* (Princeton: Princeton University Press, 1964).

8. Wen Yen Tsao, "Confucianism and Religious Tolerance," in *Chinese Philosophy,* Vol. 1: *Confucianism and Other Schools,* ed. Y. C. Koo & Others (Taipei: China Academy, 1974), pp. 73–76.

9. See Tong Fung-Wan, *Essays on Taiwanese Folk Beliefs* (Taipei: Evergreen Cultural Enterprise, 1975). This book in Chinese presents an informed attempt on the part of a Christian scholar to understand the folk religions of Taiwan. A revised and greatly enlarged edition of this book was published in 1984.

10. See Thomas Merton, *Mystics and Zen Masters* (New York: Dell Pub. Co., 1969), pp. 81–90 for an account of the Chinese Rites Controversy and the role played by the Jesuit missionary Matteo Ricci.

11. Paul Tillich, *The Future of Religions,* ed. Jerald C. Brauer (New York: Harper & Row, 1966), p. 81.

12. Ludwig Wittgenstein, *Philosophical Investigations,* tr. G. E. M. Anscombe (Oxford: Basil Blackwell & Mott, 1958), p. 82e.

13. Harvey Cox, in a lecture given at the New School for Social Research in New York City in 1968, suggested that even as various cultures have differ-

ent languages which are valid for them, so these same cultures have different religions which are also valid for them. Cox stressed the fact that there are few people who ever really think in a language other than their mother tongue and, in a similar manner, few people convert to other religions in terms of their basic view of reality.

14. Ludwig Wittgenstein, *Zettel*, ed. G. E. M. Anscombe and G. H. von Wright, tr. G. E. M. Anscombe (Oxford: Basil Blackwell, 1967), p. 26e.
15. Langdon Gilkey, *Naming the Whirlwind: The Renewal of God-Language* (Indianapolis and New York: Bobbs-Merrill, 1969), p. 20.
16. Merton, *Asian Journal*, pp. 314–315.
17. Tillich, *Theology of Culture*, p. 42.
18. Tillich, *The Future of Religions*, p. 93.
19. *Ibid.*, p. 81.
20. Mircea Eliade, "Paul Tillich and the History of Religions," in Tillich, *The Future of Religions*, pp. 31–36.
21. Karl Barth, *Christ and Adam: Man and Humanity in Romans 5*, tr. T. A. Smail (New York: Collier, 1962), p. 111.
22. Merton, *Asian Journal*, p. 315.
23. Kosuke Koyama, *Waterbuffalo Theology* (London: SCM Press, 1974), p. 130.
24. Merton, *Mystics and Zen Masters*, pp. 204–205.
25. *Ibid.*, p. 209.
26. *Ibid.*, p. 209.
27. Merton, *Asian Journal*, p. 312.
28. Thomas Merton, *Zen and the Birds of Appetite* (New York: New Directions, 1968), p. 45
29. *Ibid.*, p. 42. The book referred to is D. T. Suzuki, *Mysticism: Christian and Buddhist, The Eastern and Western Way* (New York: Macmillan, 1969).
30. Merton, *Mystics and Zen Masters*, p. 210.
31. Thomas Merton, *Contemplation in a World of Action* (Garden City: Doubleday, 1971), p. 154.
32. Thomas Merton, *The Way of Chuang Tzu* (New York: New Directions, 1965), p. 23.
33. *Ibid.*, p. 21
34. Merton, *Zen and the Birds of Appetite*, p. 54.
35. *Ibid.*, p. 30.
36. Klaus Klostermaier, *In the Paradise of Krishna: Hindu and Christian Seekers*, tr. Antonia Fonseca (Philadelphia: Westminster Press, 1969), p. 98.
37. *Ibid.*, p. 99.

4. Theology as Grammar:
Reflections on Theological Language

1. Ludwig Wittgenstein, *Tractatus Logico-Philosophicus*, tr. D. F. Pears &

B. F. McGuinness (London: Routledge & Kegan Paul, 1961), p. 115.

2. Ludwig Wittgenstein, *On Certainty,* ed. G. E. M. Anscombe & G. H. von Wright, tr. Denis Paul & G. E. M. Anscombe (New York: Harper & Row, 1969), p. 34e.

3. Wittgenstein, *Tractatus Logico-Philosophicus,* p. 51.

4. Ludwig Wittgenstein, *Philosophical Investigations,* tr. G. E. M. Anscombe (Oxford: Basil Blackwell & Mott, 1958), p. 49e.

5. *Ibid.,* p. 116e. For a discussion of Wittgenstein's views as they relate to religion and theology see Gilbert Ryle, "Ludwig Wittgenstein and the Transition to the Linguistic View," in *Ways of Understanding Religion,* ed. Walter H. Capps (New York: Macmillan, 1972), pp. 321–329; W. D. Hudson, *Ludwig Wittgenstein: The Bearing of His Philosophy Upon Religious Belief* (London: Lutterworth Press, 1968); and Alan Keightley, *Wittgenstein, Grammar and God* (London: Epworth Press, 1976).

6. Ludwig Wittgenstein, *Zettel,* ed. G. E. M. Anscombe & G. H. von Wright, tr. G. E. M. Anscombe (Oxford: Basil Blackwell, 1967), p. 12e.

7. Wittgenstein, *Philosophical Investigations,* p. 131e.

8. Wittgenstein, *Tractatus Logico-Philosophicus,* p. 45.

9. Wittgenstein, *On Certainty,* p. 17e.

10. *Ibid.,* p. 52e.

11. *Ibid.,* p. 30e.

12. *Ibid.,* p. 21e.

13. *Ibid.,* p. 31e.

14. Wittgenstein, *Zettel,* p. 26e.

15. Wittgenstein, *Philosophical Investigations,* p. 82e.

16. Wittgenstein, *Zettel,* p. 124e.

17. Wittgenstein, *Tractatus Logico-Philosophicus,* p. 151.

18. *Ibid.,* p. 151. Wittgenstein, also on page 151, sums up what he considers to be the proper method for dealing with metaphysical statements: "The correct method in philosophy would really be the following: to say nothing except what can be said, i.e. propositions of natural science—i.e. something that has nothing to do with philosophy—and then, whenever someone else wanted to say something metaphysical, to demonstrate to him that he had failed to give a meaning to certain signs in his propositions. Although it would not be satisfying to the other person—he would not have the feeling that we were teaching him philosophy—*this* method would be the only strictly correct one."

5. Toward an Adequate Interpretation of Scripture

1. Norbert Wiener, *The Human Use of Human Beings: Cybernetics and Society* (Garden City: Doubleday Anchor, 1954), p. 86.

2. Kenneth K. S. Ch'en, *Buddhism in China: A Historical Survey* (Princeton: Princeton University Press, 1964), pp. 68–69.

3. *Ibid.*, p. 69.
4. *Ibid.*, p. 116.
5. Chan Wing-Tsit, tr./compiler, *A Source Book in Chinese Philosophy* (Princeton: Princeton University Press, 1963), p. 19.
6. The following anthologies will introduce the interested reader to Asian theological thought: Gerald H. Anderson, ed. *Asian Voices in Christian Theology* (Maryknoll, New York: Orbis Books, 1976); Douglas J. Elwood, ed. *Asian Christian Theology: Emerging Themes* (Philadelphia: Westminster Press, 1980); Douglas J. Elwood, "Christian Theology in an Asian Setting: The Gospel and Chinese Intellectual Culture," *South East Asia Journal of Theology*, Vol. 16, No. 2 (1975), 1–16; John C. England, ed. *Living Theology in Asia* (London: SCM Press, 1981); and Emerito Nacpil & Douglas J. Elwood, eds. *The Human and the Holy: Asian Perspectives in Christian Theology* (Maryknoll, New York: Orbis Books, 1980).
7. See Herman Dooyeweerd, *In the Twilight of Western Thought* (Philadelphia: The Presbyterian and Reformed Publishing Company, 1960).
8. Kazoh Kitamori, *Theology of the Pain of God* (Richmond: John Knox Press, 1958).
9. Kosuke Koyama, *Waterbuffalo Theology* (London: SCM Press, 1974), p. 121.
10. Kitamori, *Theology of the Pain of God*, p. 150.
11. *Ibid.*, p. 151.
12. *Ibid.*, p. 167.
13. *Ibid.*, pp. 16–17.
14. See the following works by Kosuke Koyama: *Waterbuffalo Theology* (London: SCM Press, 1974); *Fifty Meditations* (Maryknoll, New York: Orbis Books, 1979); *No Handle on the Cross: An Asian Meditation on the Crucified Mind* (London: SCM Press, 1976); *Theology in Contact* (Madras: Christian Literature Society, 1975); and *Three Mile an Hour God* (Maryknoll, New York: Orbis Books, 1980).
15. Koyama, *Waterbuffalo Theology*, p. vii.
16. *Ibid.*, p. ix.
17. *Ibid.*, p. ix.
18. *Ibid.*, p. 129.
19. Emerito Nacpil, "Editorial: The Critical Asian Principle," *South East Asia Journal of Theology*, Vol. 17, No. 1 (1976), i.
20. *Ibid.*, pp. i–ii.
21. *Ibid.*, pp. ii–iii.

6. Culture, Philosophy, and Church Unity

1. J. Gordon Melton, *The Encylopedia of American Religions*, I (Wilmington, North Carolina: McGrath Pub. Co., 1978), pp. 109–143. In addition to the Presbyterian-Reformed bodies, there are also four Congregational bodies with Reformed theology.

2. This is not to place a value judgment on Billy Graham, Nora Lam, and Carl McIntire, but only to point out the view held by some Presbyterians in the West.

3. A classic example among American Presbyterians was the founding of Westminster Theological Seminary in 1929 by a group that left Princeton Theological Seminary because of what they perceived to be liberal theology.

4. See Jung Young Lee, "The Yin-Yang Way of Thinking," in *Asian Christian Theology: Emerging Themes,* ed. Douglas J. Elwood (Philadelphia: Westminster Press, 1980), pp. 81–88.

5. These statistics are taken from several different denominational sources in Korea. Due to new divisions that arise these statistics are in a state of continual flux.

6. Margery Wolf, *Women and the Family in Rural Taiwan* (Stanford: Stanford University Press, 1972), pp. viii–ix.

7. We are speaking here in a strictly cultural sense. These comments are not to be understood politically. In the words of Wolf, *Women and the Family in Rural Taiwan,* p. ix: "My insistence on the Chineseness of the Taiwanese should in no way be construed as a political statement." It should be noted that the so-called Mountain People or aborigines trace their ancestry to areas of the South Pacific and Malayasia. However, they are greatly influenced by the dominant culture of Taiwan, that of the Chinese.

8. Louis J. Luzbetak, *The Church and Cultures* (Techny, Illinois: Divine Word Publications, 1963), p. 114.

9. David J. Hesselgrave, *Communicating Christ Cross-Culturally* (Grand Rapids: Zondervan, 1978), pp. 202–203.

10. Wing-Tsit Chan, "The Story of Chinese Philosophy," in *The Chinese Mind: Essentials of Chinese Philosophy and Culture,* ed. Charles A. Moore (Honolulu: East-West Center Press, 1967), p. 54.

11. *Ibid.,* p. 53.

12. See Lee, "The Yin-Yang Way of Thinking," pp. 81–86. See also Jung Young Lee, *The Theology of Change: A Christian Concept of God in an Eastern Perspective* (Maryknoll, New York: Orbis Books, 1979).

13. Fung Yu-Lan, *A Short History of Chinese Philosophy,* ed. Derk Bodde (New York: Macmillan, 1948), p. 12.

14. See, for example, Choan-Seng Song, "The Seed of Hope in the Womb," *Religious Education,* Vol. 74, No. 5 (September-October 1979), 533–542.

15. Hajime Nakamura, *Ways of Thinking of Eastern Peoples: India, China, Tibet, Japan,* rev. & ed. Philip P. Wiener (Honolulu: East-West Center Press, 1964), p. 190.

16. While a graduate student at a university in Taiwan in 1977–1979 the author encountered a strange situation whereby both semesters of the course in Chinese philosophy were taught by foreigners. This was partially due to the fact that the younger students in philosophy would rather study western philosophy than Chinese philosophy. Hopefully there will be those of the

younger generation who will seek to know and build upon the Chinese philosophical heritage.

17. John S. Mbiti, "Theological Impotence and the Universality of the Church," in *Mission Trends No. 3: Third World Theologies*, ed. Gerald H. Anderson & Thomas F. Stransky (New York and Grand Rapids: Paulist Press/Eerdmans, 1976), p. 8.
18. Norman L. Geisler, "Some Philosophical Perspectives on Missionary Dialogue," in *Theology and Mission*, ed. David J. Hesselgrave (Grand Rapids: Baker, 1978), p. 242.

7. Theological Method: Four Contemporary Models

1. See Daniel J. Adams, "Theological Method: Four Contemporary Models," *Taiwan Journal of Theology*, No. 3 (March 1981), 193–205.
2. Cornelius Van Til, for example, made a trip to Asia in the 1950s and visited Taiwan Theological College. A signed copy of his syllabus *Christian Theistic Ethics* (1958) is in the library as a memento of that visit.
3. See Herman Dooyeweerd, *A New Critique of Theoretical Thought*, tr. David H. Freeman, William S. Young & H. De Jongste, 4 vols. (Amsterdam: H. J. Paris and Philadelphia: Presbyterian and Reformed, 1953–1958).
4. Antony Flew & Alasdair Macintyre, ed., *New Essays in Philosophical Theology* (New York: Macmillan, 1964). See also Ian T. Ramsey, *Religious Language: An Empirical Placing of Theological Phrases* (New York: Macmillan, 1963).
5. A blending of theoria and praxis within the Asian context is found in Emerito P. Nacpil & Douglas J. Elwood, eds., *The Human and the Holy: Asian Perspectives in Christian Theology* (Maryknoll, New York: Orbis Books, 1980).
6. G. C. Berkouwer's *Studies in Dogmatics* have appeared as follows:
   Faith and Sanctification, tr. John Vriend (1952)
   The Providence of God, tr. Lewis B. Smedes (1952)
   Faith and Justification, tr. Lewis B. Smedes (1954)
   The Person of Christ, tr. John Vriend (1955)
   General Revelation (1955)
   Faith and Perseverance, tr. Robert D. Knudsen (1958)
   Divine Election, tr. Hugo Bekker (1960)
   Man: The Image of God, tr. Dirk W. Jellema (1962)
   The Work of Christ, tr. Cornelius Lambregtse (1965)
   The Sacraments, tr. Hugo Bekker (1969)
   Sin, tr. Philip C. Holtrop (1971)
   The Return of Christ (1972)
   Holy Scripture, tr./ed. Jack B. Rogers (1975)
   The Church, tr. James E. Davison (1976).
   All are published by Eerdmans in Grand Rapids. See also G. C. Berkou-

wer, *A Half Century of Theology: Movements and Motives*, tr. & ed. Lewis B. Smedes (Grand Rapids: Eerdmans, 1977).

7. See G. C. Berkouwer, *The Triumph of Grace in the Theology of Karl Barth*, tr. Harry R. Boer (Grand Rapids: Eerdmans, 1956) and G. C. Berkouwer, *The Second Vatican Council and the New Catholicism*, tr. Lewis B. Smedes (Grand Rapids: Eerdmans, 1965).

8. For a concise summary of Berkouwer's theology see Lewis B. Smedes, "G. C. Berkouwer," in *Creative Minds in Contemporary Theology*, ed. Philip Edgcumbe Hughes (Grand Rapids: Eerdmans, 1966), pp. 63–97.

9. See John B. Cobb, Jr., "Buddhism and Christianity as Complementary," *Northeast Asia Journal of Theology*, Nos. 20/21 (March/September 1978), 19–30. A dialogue between Cobb and Seiichi Yagi follows in the same issue, 31–52.

10. John B. Cobb, Jr. & David Ray Griffin, *Process Theology: An Introductory Exposition* (Philadelphia: Westminster Press, 1976) and David Ray Griffin & Thomas J. J. Altizer, eds., *John Cobb's Theology in Process* (Philadelphia: Westminster Press, 1977).

11. Robert McAfee Brown, *Theology in a New Key: Responding to Liberation Themes* (Philadelphia: Westminster Press, 1978).

12. C. S. Song, *Christian Mission in Reconstruction: An Asian Attempt* (Madras: Christian Literature Society, 1976); *Third-Eye Theology: Theology in Formation in Asian Settings* (Maryknoll, New York: Orbis Books, 1979); and *The Compassionate God* (Maryknoll, New York: Orbis Books, 1982). See also the following books by C. S. Song, *The Tears of Lady Meng: A Parable of People's Political Theology* (Geneva: World Council of Churches, 1981) and *Tell Us Our Names: A Story Theology from an Asian Perspective* (Maryknoll, New York: Orbis Books, 1984).

13. C. S. Song, "From Israel to Asia: A Theological Leap," in *European Theology Challenged by the World-Wide Church*, Occasional Paper No. 8 (Geneva: Conference of European Churches, 1976), pp. 10–29.

14. See "Reviewing and Responding to the Thought of Choan-Seng Song," *Occasional Bulletin of Missionary Research*, Vol. 1, No. 3 (July 1977), 9–15. Song's reply is found on pp. 13–15.

15. Jung Young Lee, *The Theology of Change: A Christian Concept of God in an Eastern Perspective* (Maryknoll, New York: Orbis Books, 1979).

8. The Importance of Christian Myth

1. Guilford Dudley III, *The Recovery of Christian Myth* (Philadelphia: Westminster Press, 1967), p. 19.

2. Rudolf Bultmann, "New Testament and Mythology," in *Kerygma and Myth: A Theological Debate*, ed. Hans Werner Bartsch (London: SPCK, 1957), p. 1.

3. *Ibid.*, p. 3.

4. *Ibid.*, p. 3.
5. *Ibid.*, p. 11.
6. Clyde S. Kilby, "Mythic and Christian Elements in Tolkien," in *Myth, Allegory, and Gospel*, ed. John W. Montgomery (Minneapolis: Bethany Fellowship, 1974), p. 120.
7. Dudley, *The Recovery of Christian Myth*, p. 18.
8. Alan W. Watts, *Myth and Ritual in Christianity* (Boston: Beacon Press, 1968), p. 7.
9. *Ibid.*, p. 8.
10. C. S. Lewis, *An Experiment in Criticism* (Cambridge: Cambridge University Press, 1961), p. 41.
11. See the following for a discussion of the influence of C. S. Lewis in Asia: Paul Clasper, "C. S. Lewis and the Chinese," *Ching Feng*, Vol. XX, No. 1 (1977), 61–62 and Peter K. H. Lee, "A Rejoinder," 63–69. See also Paul Clasper, "C. S. Lewis's Contribution to a Missionary Theology: An Asian Perspective," *Ching Feng*, Vol. XXIV, No. 4 (1981), p. 203–214. This article also appears in *South East Asia Journal of Theology*, Vol. 23, No. 1 (1982), 75–82.
12. Lewis, *An Experiment in Criticism*, pp. 43–44.
13. *Ibid.*, p. 43.
14. *Ibid.*, p. 44.
15. *Ibid.*, p. 44.
16. *Ibid.*, p. 44.
17. *Ibid.*, p. 44.
18. Brevard S. Childs, *Myth and Reality in the Old Testament* (London: SCM Press, 1962), p. 19.
19. Watts, *Myth and Ritual in Christianity*, p. 2.
20. See Dudley, *The Recovery of Christian Myth*, p. 15, where he states: "To say that a mythic consciousness is necessary to appreciate or understand the resurrection is not to imply a denial of its historicity. But it is to say that as a historical event the Easter event compelled its witnesses to envision the horizons of time and space into which it reached."
21. J. R. R. Tolkien, "On Fairy Stories," in *Essays Presented to Charles Williams*, ed. C. S. Lewis (Grand Rapids: Eerdmans, 1966), p. 83.
22. Dudley, *The Recovery of Christian Myth*, p. 115.
23. C. G. Jung, "The Phenomenology of the Spirit in Fairy Tales," in *Spirit and Nature: Papers from the Eranos Yearbooks*, Bollingen Series XXX: I, ed. Joseph Campbell (Princeton: Princeton University Press, 1954), p. 48.
24. Dudley, *The Recovery of Christian Myth*, p. 118.

9. The Rational and the Mystical
in Theological Construction

1. Wing-Tsit Chan, "Syntheses in Chinese Metaphysics," in *The Chinese*

Mind: Essentials of Chinese Philosophy and Culture, ed. Charles A. Moore (Honolulu: East-West Center Press, 1967), p. 132.

2. Joseph Needham, *Science and Civilization in China*, II: *History of Scientific Thought* (Cambridge: Cambridge University Press, 1956), p. 9.
3. *Ibid.*, p. 36.
4. Fung Yu-Lan, *A Short History of Chinese Philosophy*, ed. Derk Bodde (New York: Macmillan, 1948), p. 19.
5. Wing-Tsit Chan, tr./compiler, *A Source Book in Chinese Philosophy* (Princeton: Princeton University Press, 1963), p. 244.
6. *Ibid.*, p. 246.
7. See Herman Dooyeweerd, *Roots of Western Culture: Pagan, Secular, and Christian Options*, tr. John Kraay, ed. Mark Vander Vennen & Bernard Zylstra (Toronto: Wedge Publishing Foundation, 1979), pp. 7–28; L. Kalsbeek, *Contours of a Christian Philosophy: An Introduction to Herman Dooyeweerd's Thought*, tr. Judy A. Peterson, ed. Bernard & Josina Zylstra (Toronto: Wedge Publishing Foundation, 1975), pp. 62–66; and J. M. Spier, *An Introduction to Christian Philosophy*, second edition, tr. David Hugh Freeman (Philadelphia: Presbyterian and Reformed Pub. Co., 1966) pp. 24–28.
8. See Dooyeweerd, *Roots of Western Culture*, pp. 28–39.
9. See G. C. Berkouwer, *Man: The Image of God* (Studies in Dogmatics), tr. Dirk W. Jellema (Grand Rapids: Eerdmans, 1962), pp. 211–223, 255–265.
10. See "Hegelianism," in *Dictionary of Philosophy*, ed. Dagobert D. Runes (New York: Philosophical Library, 1965), pp. 123–124. This method may provide a clue as to why Barth does not consider evil to be ontological. For a critique of Barth's view of evil see David Ray Griffin, *God, Power, and Evil: A Process Theodicy* (Philadelphia: Westminster Press, 1976), pp. 150–173.
11. This is, of course, yet another dualism. For a critique of mysticism see Donald G. Bloesch, *The Ground of Certainty: Toward an Evangelical Theology of Revelation* (Grand Rapids: Eerdmans, 1971), pp. 140–155.
12. See Alan W. Watts' two books *Behold the Spirit: A Study in the Necessity of Mystical Religion* (New York: Vintage Books, 1971) and *Beyond Theology: The Art of Godmanship* (New York: Vintage Books, 1964).
13. C. K. Yang, *Religion in Chinese Society* (Berkeley/Los Angeles: University of California Press, 1961), pp. 5–6. See also Hu Shih, *The Development of the Logical Method in Ancient China*, second edition (New York: Paragon, 1968).
14. Yang, *Religion in Chinese Society*, p. 6.
15. *Ibid.*, pp. 19–20.
16. See Wolfhart Pannenberg, *Theology and the Philosophy of Science*, tr. Francis McDonagh (Philadelphia: Westminster Press, 1976) and Thomas F. Torrance, *Theological Science* (Oxford/New York/London: Oxford University Press, 1969). Pannenberg's work is described on the dust jacket as "a detailed and sustained defense of his belief that theology is a rational enter-

prise concerned with establishing the truth of theological propositions."

17. See John W. Beardslee, III, ed./tr., *Reformed Dogmatics* (Grand Rapids: Baker Book House, 1977), and Heinrich Heppe, *Reformed Dogmatics: Set Out and Illustrated from the Sources,* rev. & ed. Ernst Bizer, tr. G. T. Thompson (Grand Rapids: Baker Book House, 1978). Heppe's volume had a great influence upon Karl Barth, so much so that he wrote the Foreword to the 1935 edition. Reformed Scholasticism reached its full development in Francis Turretin (1623–1687), whose *Institutio Theologicae Elencticae,* published in 1674, became the standard theology text at Princeton Seminary until it was later replaced by Charles Hodge's *Systematic Theology.* Hodge based his work largely upon that of Turretin.

18. See Charles Hodge, *Systematic Theology,* 3 vols. (Grand Rapids: Eerdmans, 1979); Robert L. Dabney, *Lectures in Systematic Theology* (Grand Rapids: Zondervan, 1972); Jack B. Rogers & Donald K. McKim, *The Authority and Interpretation of the Bible: An Historical Approach* (San Francisco: Harper & Row, 1979); and John C. Vander Stelt, *Philosophy and Scripture: A Study in Old Princeton and Westminster Theology* (Marlton, New Jersey: Mack Publ. Co., 1978).

19. See Emily M. Ahern, *The Cult of the Dead in a Chinese Village* (Stanford: Stanford University Press, 1973); David K. Jordan, *Gods, Ghosts, and Ancestors: Folk Religion in a Chinese Village* (Berkeley/Los Angeles: University of California Press, 1972); and Arthur P. Wolf, ed., *Religion and Ritual in Chinese Society* (Stanford: Stanford University Press, 1974).

20. Justus Freytag, *The Church in Villages of Taiwan: The Impact of Modern Society and Folk Religion on Rural Churches* (Tainan: Research Center, Tainan Theological College, 1969), p. 96.

21. Laurence G. Thompson, *Chinese Religion: An Introduction,* second edition (Belmont, California: Dickenson Publ. Co., 1975), p. 3.

22. Carl Sagan, *The Dragons of Eden: Speculations on the Evolution of Human Intelligence* (New York: Random House, 1977), p. 169. For an extensive discussion of intelligence, both human and artificial, see Douglas R. Hofstader, *Gödel, Escher, Bach: An Eternal Golden Braid* (New York: Basic Books, 1979).

23. Sagan, *The Dragons of Eden,* pp. 168–169.

24. Robert J. Smith, "Afterword," in *Religion and Ritual in China,* ed. Arthur P. Wolf (Stanford: Stanford University Press, 1975), p. 105.

25. Sagan, *The Dragons of Eden,* p. 180.

26. Gary Zukav, *The Dancing Wu Li Masters: An Overview of the New Physics* (New York: William Morrow, 1979), p. 309. See also Fritjof Capra, *The Tao of Physics: An Exploration of the Parallels Between Modern Physics and Eastern Mysticism* (New York: Bantam Books, 1975) and Werner Heisenberg, *Physics and Philosophy* (New York: Harper & Row, 1958).

27. Zukav, *The Dancing Wu Li Masters,* p. 286.

28. *Ibid.,* p. 298.

29. *Ibid.,* p. 315.

30. Note that we refer to a universal and transcultural *theology;* not a universal and transcultural *religion.*
31. Zukav, *The Dancing Wu Li Masters,* p. 23.
32. John Calvin, *Calvin:/Theological Treatises,* Library of Christian Classics, XXII, tr. J. K. S. Reid (Philadelphia: Westminster Press, n.d.), p. 171.
33. *Ibid.,* p. 172.
34. *Ibid.,* pp. 173–174.
35. John Calvin, *Institutes of the Christian Religion,* II, Library of Christian Classics, XXI, ed. John T. McNeill, tr. Ford Lewis Battles (Philadelphia: Westminster Press, 1960), p. 1416.
36. Calvin, *Theological Treatises,* p. 49.
37. *Ibid.,* p. 310.
38. *Ibid.,* p. 153.
39. Calvin, *Institutes of the Christian Religion,* II, p. 1422.
40. Hendrikus Berkhof, *Christian Faith: An Introduction to the Study of the Faith,* tr. Sierd Woudstra (Grand Rapids: Eerdmans, 1979), p. 389.
41. Karl Barth, *Church Dogmatics,* IV/4, Fragment, tr. G. W. Bromiley, ed. G. W. Bromiley & T. F. Torrance (Edinburgh: T. & T. Clark, 1969), p. 103.
42. G. C. Berkouwer, *The Sacraments,* tr. Hugo Bekker (Grand Rapids: Eerdmans, 1969), p. 49.
43. Berkhof, *Christian Faith,* p. 57.
44. See Arthur P. Wolf, "Gods, Ghosts, and Ancestors," in *Religion and Ritual in Chinese Society,* ed. Arthur P. Wolf (Stanford: Stanford University Press, 1974), pp. 176–177 for a discussion of the symbolism of eating in Chinese society. See Choan-Seng Song, *Third-Eye Theology: Theology in Formation in Asian Settings* (Maryknoll, New York: Orbis Books, 1979), pp. 141–157, where, in a masterpiece of contextual theology, he interprets the Lord's Supper as the sacramental meaning of memory, thus relating it to the veneration of ancestors. For an interpretation of the Lord's Supper from the perspective of liberation theology see Tissa Balasuriya, *The Eucharist and Human Liberation* (Maryknoll, New York: Orbis Books, 1977).

10. A Look to the Future

1. Tissa Balasuriya, *Planetary Theology* (Maryknoll, New York: Orbis Books, 1984), p. 14.
2. Paul Tillich, *The Future of Religions,* ed. Jerald C. Brauer (New York: Harper & Row, 1966), p. 81.
3. See John Hick, *God Has Many Names* (Philadelphia: Westminster Press, 1982); Ninian Smart, *Worldviews: Crosscultural Explorations in Human Beliefs* (New York: Scribners, 1983); and Wilfred C. Smith, *Towards a World Theology: Faith and the Comparative History of Religion* (Philadelphia: Westminster Press, 1981).

4. Balasuriya's book approaches planetary theology from the perspective of an integrated theological and sociological approach. This is the first such work from Asia, usually associated with contextual theologies. For a view from the perspective of contextual theology see Robert J. Schreiter, *Constructing Local Theologies* (Maryknoll, New York: Orbis Books, 1985).

5. Lam Wing-hung, "Patterns of Chinese Theology" in *The Bible and Theology in Asian Contexts: An Evangelical Perspective on Asian Theology*, eds. Bong Rin Ro & Ruth Eshenaur (Taichung, Taiwan: Asia Theological Association, 1984), p. 339.

6. Balasuriya, *Planetary Theology*, p. 15.

7. Nicholls, Bruce, "A Living Theology for Asian Churches: Some Reflections on the Contextualization-Syncretism Debate" in *The Bible and Theology in Asian Contexts: An Evangelical Perspective on Asian Theology*, eds. Bong Rin Ro & Ruth Eshenaur (Taichung, Taiwan: Asia Theological Association, 1984), p. 134.